D0901086

Private Prayers
and
Public Parades

— Exploring the Religious Life of Taipei

Department of Information, Taipei City Government

Publisher: Wu Yu-sheng
Editor-in-chief: Kao Li-fung
Executive Editors: Jiang Chuen-heuy, Ouyang Pei-szu
Consultant: Cheng Chi-ming
English Editor: Rick Charette
Writer & Photographer: Mark Caltionhill
Art Designer: Wang Cheng-hung
Marketing and Circulation: Tsai Tsung-hau, Chou Tien-yung

Published by: Department of Information, Taipei City Government
Address: 4F, No.1, ShiFu Road, Taipei
Tel: (02) 2728-7564
Fax: (02) 2720-5909

Printer: Yun Xin Color Printing Co., Ltd.   **Tel:** (02) 2248-3436
Publishing Date: December, 2002

All rights reserved; no part of this publication may be reproduced or transmitted by any means, electronic, mechanical, photocopying or otherwise, without the prior permission of the publisher.

Unified Number: 1009105323
ISBN: 957-01-3260-4
Price: NT$200

Contents

Foreword by Mayor Ma Ying-jeou

Making Taipei a truly international city has been one of the main policies pursued by the city government over the last four years. This effort can be divided into two parts: taking Taipei to the world and bringing the world to Taipei. Through commissioning this book, we hope to advance both of these causes.

A second key element underlying many, if not all, of the city administration's initiatives is modernization. This in no way implies abandonment of the past or the whole-scale adoption of alien values but, instead, a process of moving forward by combining the best of the past with the best for the future. Given Taipei's rich and diverse cultural resources, to do otherwise would be foolish.

While many aspects of culture are subtle or hidden from sight, a visitor spending any length of time here cannot fail to become aware of the numerous strata of religious experiences taking place at almost every moment, from the noisy street celebrations of Daoist gods, through the elegant rituals of Confucianism, to the silent contemplation of Buddhist practice.

This conspicuousness does not equate necessarily to easy understanding, however, and even long-term foreign residents of the city may not know to whom it is that locals make offerings and light incense, how ancestor worship and veneration of gods can be practiced in harmony, why taxi drivers plaster their cabs with swastikas and so on.

The wide range of topics covered and in depth introductions to background theories make this book an essential starting point for anyone wishing to understand the grassroots culture that is Taipei's heartbeat.

Ma Ying-jeou
Taipei City Mayor
December 2002

Preface

Like many writers perhaps, I have written the book I wished to read, a kind I have not yet found in the island's bookstores. What I wanted was an accessible guidebook to Taipei. Not to its sights and buildings, however, but to its customs and practices.

Living in a culture so different from the one in which I grew up, not a day goes by that at least one question does not present itself. Finding answers has not always proved straightforward nor, unfortunately, always accurate. This is particularly true of aspects of local religion, where the reasons for many practices may even be forgotten by the people practicing them. Moreover, there cannot be many subjects on which as much spurious information has been published in English as has been about "Daoism" and "Chinese folk religion." Hopefully, the present volume does not add to this.

My thanks are due to Professor Cheng Chih-ming of Fu Ren Catholic University for content editing, to Rick Charette for English editing, to Phoebe Ouyang, as ever, for her reserves of patience during editing, and to Wang Neng-yu for providing photos for those festivals I missed during my stay in Taiwan.

Thanks to Dharma Master Liao-yi and Master Bao-hsiang for help with Buddhist concepts, and to many, including Jocelyn Chuo, at the Museum of World Religions for help in sorting through Chinese-language materials relating to popular religious practice. Thanks also to everyone who has been unfortunate enough to sit near me in a coffee shop when I've been translating, never expecting to be asked, "Excuse me, what does this mean?"

Most importantly, however, thanks to Charlotte Fan, who shared my passion for this project and who made invaluable contributions at all stages. Without her, this book would not exist and my time in Taiwan would have been very different.

Mark Caltonhill
Taipei, December 2002

Summary of Main Chinese Dynasties

Legendary Period		3rd millennium BCE
Xia	夏	c. 21st-16th centuries BCE
Shang (Yin)	商	c. 16th-11th centuries BCE
Zhou (Including Warring States Period)	周 戰國	c.11th century - 221 BCE 475-221 BCE)
Qin	秦	221-206 BCE
Han	漢	206 BCE - 220 CE
Epoch of the Three Kingdoms	三國	220-280 CE
Western Jin	西晉	265-316 CE
Eastern Jin	東晉	317- 420 CE
Northern and Southern Dynasties	南北朝	420-581 CE
Sui	隋	581-618 CE
Tang (唐; 618-907)	唐	618-907 CE
Five Dynasties	五代	907-960 CE
Song	宋	960-1279 CE
Yuan	元	1279/1-1368 CE
Ming	明	1368-1644 CE
Qing	清	1644-1911 CE
Republican Period (Peoples' Republic on mainland)	中華民國	1912 - (1949- CE)

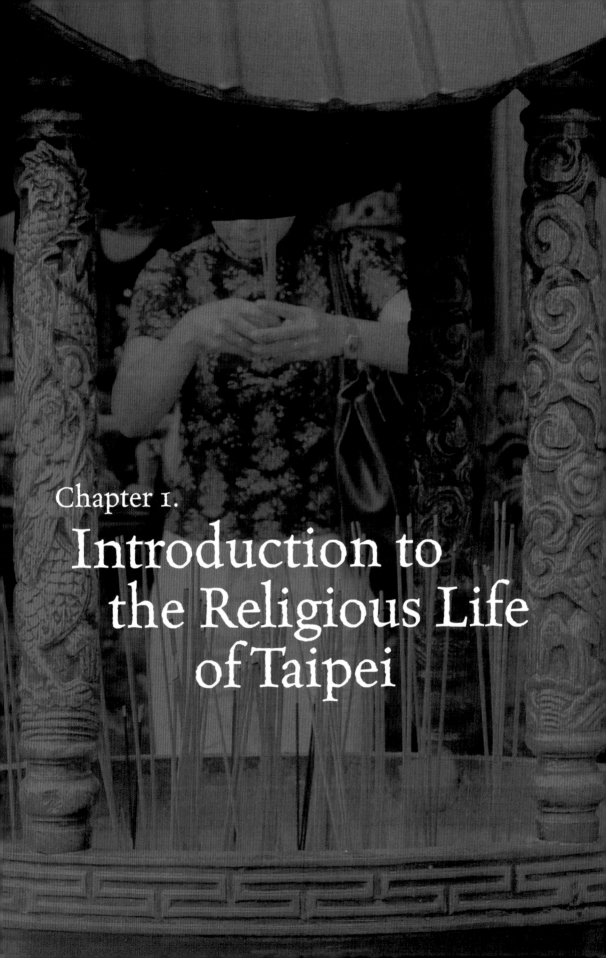

Chapter 1.
Introduction to the Religious Life of Taipei

Three Religions and Popular Religious Practice

Han-Chinese, who form the vast majority of Taipei's population, tend to say they are a people of "Three Religions" (三教). These are identified as Confucianism (儒教), Daoism (道教) and Buddhism (佛教).

This book is about all three, yet about none of them. After a brief introduction to each in this chapter, these formal religions will rarely appear again.

This is not to say that these religions are not important in the lives of many Taipei citizens but, rather, that the day-to-day religious practices seen around the city really belong to a "folk" or "popular" tradition that runs alongside, beneath or above these Three Religions.

Teachings of the Ancestors

A first problem in exploring Taipei's religious life in English is language. The Chinese word *jiao* (教) really means "teachings," and, under Western influence, around one hundred years ago, was combined with *zong* (宗; ancestor) to create a new word *zong-jiao* equivalent to the Western word "religion."

While "ancestor teachings" captures the essential nature of Chinese religion, it suggests a separation between religion and other aspects of life that has never existed in Chinese society. What we define as religion is merely an integral part of everyday life, in which it is believed that a person's existence, powers and influence, although diminished after death, are no less real than they were before.

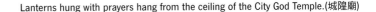

Lanterns hung with prayers hang from the ceiling of the City God Temple.(城隍廟)

More recently, the word *xin-yang* (信仰; belief) has gained circulation, but some authorities still find this inadequate as Chinese religion is characterized as much by practice, custom and ritual as by belief.

Practices, Customs and Rituals

This book, while not negating the importance of orthodox schools of the Three Religions, focuses attention on the daily, monthly and annual practices that characterize traditional religious life in the city. For convenience, these are designated as "folk" or "popular" beliefs (民間信仰), though yet again this title is not entirely satisfactory.

Furthermore, these "beliefs" are interwoven intimately with aspects of the Three Religions. Statues of the "Buddhist" bodhisattva Guanyin (觀音) are found in "Daoist" temples throughout the city; fruit and flowers pile up before statues of Confucius each time exams loom, and wooden divinatory blocks (筊杯) can be found in "Buddhist" temples and monasteries, even though, in its purer forms, Buddhism has no deities or spirits that can be consulted.

A "popular" group will also avail of Buddhist monastics' and Daoist priests' knowledge of rituals and scriptures, in order to evoke the presence and power of spirits and deities.

In light of these interactions between "popular" religious practices and "orthodox" schools, before looking at religious aspects of everyday life (chapter two), annual festivities (chapter three), temple life (chapter four) and so forth, this introduction will conclude with a brief look at each of the Three Religions.

Depiction of Confucius traveling from state to state.

1. Confucianism

Usually translated as "Confucianism," the Chinese term *Ru-jiao* (儒教) does not bear his name and means something like "Scholar's Teachings." A.C. Graham* suggests that the term predated Confucius himself and, originally meaning "soft," the word *ru* was probably applied by men who ruled and waged war to the "softies" who merely taught.

By the end of the "age of philosophers" which accompanied the collapse of Zhou dynasty control and the increasing competition between the "warring states," *Ru* was one of various competing systems of thought and, although listed as one of the main Six Schools at the end of the 2nd century BCE, the *ru* were not really philosophers but professional teachers, the preservers of ancient traditions.

---

* A.C. Graham, *Disputers of the Tao*, 1989, p. 31

Tradition is preserved at the Confucian birthday celebrations.

They taught that which was not practicably "useful," known later as the Six Arts (六藝), comprising ceremony, music, archery, chariot driving, writing and mathematics. By the Han dynasty, the written curriculum composed the Six Classics recording the heights of Zhou dynasty civilization. These were the *Book of Documents* (書經; proclamations of Zhou and pre-Zhou rulers), *Book of Odes* (詩經; anthology of early Zhou verses), *Spring and Autumn Annals* (春秋; history of Confucius's home state of Lu), *Book of Changes* (易經; manual of divination), *Book of Rites* (禮經; Han commentary on traditional rituals) and the *Book of Music* (樂經).

Whilst claiming to devote itself to political and practical problems of the earthly realm, and not to "speak of marvels, feats of strength, disorder [of nature] or spirits,"* Confucianism also concerned itself with the correct practice of ancestral ritual.

Official Educators

Far from being a religion, Confucianism was really aimed at preparing the sons of nobility for public office. By the Han dynasty, these teachers had a lineage traceable back to Confucius (孔夫子; trad. 551-479 BCE) and his disciples, and, after establishment of a government bureaucracy chosen through examination, Confucianism became an orthodox teaching system, albeit colored by the

---

* 論語 (*The Analects of Confucius*), Chapter VII, verse 21.

A Daoist priest is often on hand at temples to perform impromptu rituals.

A Daoist priest's clothing, instruments and divination tools lying ready for use.

austerity of the Legalists (法家).

Influence of the *Ru* school ebbed and flowed as the examination system disappeared following collapse of the Han (220 CE), reappeared with the Sui and Tang (6th-8th centuries), and finally blossomed as Neo-Confucianism in the Song dynasty (10th-13th centuries) albeit under the religious influence of Buddhism.

This decline of Buddhism and rise of Confucianism occurred only in an educated minority, however; the mass of the people continued their religious beliefs unaffected and, to some extent, subsumed Confucianism's religious dimension.

Today, Confucian temples are still found in every major city in Taiwan and his birthday is celebrated on September 28th. Moreover, it was only through a negative vote in the legislature during the early years of the ROC that Confucianism did not become the country's state religion.

2. Daoism

While it is usual to distinguish between Philosophic Daoism and Religious Daoism, there is no clear distinction between religion and philosophy in Chinese thought, and the later religious schools made use of the earlier teachings of Lao-zi (老子) and Zhuang-zi (莊子), as well as promoting Lao-zi as a major deity.

These philosophic teachings in turn, expressing many ideas handed down from ancient Chinese thinking, centered around living in harmony with the *Dao* (道; Way), which led to esoteric methods of attaining long life and immortality.

Religious Daoism emerged from two movements towards the end of the Han dynasty. One, based on the revelations of Zhang Dao-ling (張道陵; c.142 CE) offered a way of salvation through repentance, healing and spells, and created an organized form of Daoism from the mass of popular practices. His school, the Way of the Heavenly Master (天師道), was also known as Five Pecks of Rice Daoism (五斗米教) from the joining fee. The first imperial sacrifices to Lao-zi were offered in 165 CE.

The second movement, that of Great Peace Daoism (太平道) was less influential in the long run but helped lead to the collapse of the Han dynasty by giving rise to the Yellow Turban Revolt (黃巾之亂) of 184 CE.

During the disunity which followed and the increase in Buddhist influence in China, Daoism developed its doctrines (such as ideas about the afterlife) and a monastic organization, as well as "scientific" aspects such as *feng-shui* (風水) and *yin-yang* (陰陽), and divination using the *Book of Changes,* which created links with Confucianism.

Indeed, during the Tang dynasty, there was a general doctrinal and liturgical synthesis between Daoism and Buddhism and Confucianism.

The numerous buddha statues depict the concept that every creature has a buddha-nature waiting to be discovered.

Daoism in the Song dynasty saw the appearance of numerous new schools including the Supreme Unity (太一), Perfect and Great Way (真大道), Complete Perfection (全真) and Orthodox Unity (正一), the latter a direct successor of Zhang's Heavenly Master school. Different schools emphasized different texts, different approaches to seeking immortality, different rituals and so forth.

Daoism in Taiwan is still characterized by its numerous schools, though all acknowledge Zhang Dao-ling's role as founding patriarch.

It should be remembered, however, that no one will ever describe themselves as a believer in "popular religion," which is merely an academic appellation. Most people saying they are Daoist (or often Buddhist for that matter) may have little or no connection with any formal school.

3. Buddhism

It is not clear when Buddhists or Buddhist ideas first entered China, but by around 150 CE, missionary monks had established a center for study and translation at Luoyang (洛陽), the imperial capital.

Although both Theravada and Mahayana texts and techniques were introduced, and were of great interest to Chinese because of similarities with indigenous practices and the philosophies of Lao-zi and Zhuang-zi, nevertheless the translations were poor and had there been no further contact, Buddhism would probably have become merely a school of Daoism.

Decline of the Han dynasty towards the end of the 2nd century CE offered a great opportunity to Buddhism, which appealed more to the common people than did Confucianism. It also taught that salvation was available to everyone, giving them the tools of meditation and moral discipline, as well as compassionate deities such as Guanyin and the Amitha Buddha. For the scholar class it offered a more developed philosophy than that of Daoism.

During the four centuries of disunity that followed, many missionaries and new texts arrived from the west. Translation methods also improved as groups of disciples concentrated on a single text (often taking the sutra's name for that of their sect), without altogether ignoring the efforts of other groups.

Reunification under the Sui and then Tang produced a great creative mixing of all that had been happening over the previous years. Chinese Buddhism blossomed, with support in all classes, and thousands of monasteries and temples were built. The initial period of misinterpretation, which had been succeeded by correct interpretation, now gave way to creative reinterpretation.

Ultimately, ten schools came to the fore; five were essentially transplanted from India, five were Chinese developments. The four most important, all Chinese innovations, were the Tian-tai (天臺), Hua-yan (華嚴), Zen (禪) and Jing-tu (淨土; Pureland).

Zen, which stressed meditative practice, was a reaction to excessive emphasis on scriptural study; Pureland appealed to those who found philosophy or meditation too demanding or for whom the chaos of the times gave little hope.

Severe persecution by the Daoist Tang emperor Wu Zong (武宗) in 845 led to destruction of 46,000 monasteries, return of 265,000 monastics to secular life, and destruction of statues and scriptures.

The emperor's death two years later was not soon enough to save most schools, and only Zen (because it did not rely on statues and scriptures) and Pureland (because of its popular support) really survived independently, though elements of the other schools were absorbed by them or were preserved in Japan and Korea.

Although the Song emperors were favorable towards Buddhism, its intellectual golden age was over. The Zen and Pureland schools became ever more similar, such that today's Taiwanese Buddhist groups are essentially a syncretism of both schools. Early ROC intolerance towards many traditional aspects of culture is long gone, and Buddhism flourishes in Taiwan with one of the highest monastic populations in the world.

Buddhist statue wearing a Five Buddha Crown.

Indigenous Religion
—Beliefs and Practices among
Taipei's Aborigines

Wall mosaic depicting ancestral spirit ceremony in an Aboriginal township near Taipei.

Until some four centuries ago, the Chinese were only vaguely aware of Taiwan's existence even though it lies only some hundred and fifty kilometers off the southwest coast. Taiwan's indigenous peoples still represented 98% of the population and many of the Chinese were seasonal traders.

There were then some two-dozen ethnic groups, belonging to the Austronesian-speaking Language Group (which includes peoples as diverse as Madagascar, New Zealand, Easter Island and Hawaii), each with its distinct language, customs and social structure. At times they traded with each other; at other times they fought.

Today, the situation is reversed, with less 2% of Taiwan's people being registered as Aborigine (原住民), although many more are of mixed race.

Tribes of the Taipei Basin

The local Plains Aborigines (平埔族) were subject to such political and cultural pressure from the immigrating Han-Chinese that these ethnic groups have, to all intents, been assimilated into mainstream culture. Their centuries of habitation are now best remembered in a few place names for which the Chinese equivalents make little sense, such as Chi-li-an (唭哩岸), Guandu (關渡) or Beitou

(北投), or in physical reminders of their struggle with the Chinese settlers such as the stone boundary marker preserved at Shi-pai (石牌; Stone Marker) MRT station.

The few Aborigines in Taipei today, therefore, are not so much the original Plains Aborigines but representatives of all the island's extant groups, drawn to Taipei for work, study or love.

Christians and Animists

Furthermore, even the ten or so mountain-, coast- and island-dwelling groups who better resisted sinicization became a major target of Christian missionary work, to the extent that now more than 95% of Taiwan's indigenous people's profess membership of one or another church. Before conversion, they, rather like the Han-Chinese, believed in an assortment of deities, ghosts, ancestral souls, good and evil spirits, and other supernatural forces. Discerning the will or sentiments of these spirits was necessary before important tasks could take place or for diagnosing the causes of an illness or social problem.

Their belief systems, although different for each ethnic group, can be divided into two main categories. These are the *kawas* system of the Paiwan, Rukai, Amis, Puyuma, and Ketagalan (one of the Plains groups in the Taipei area), and *anito* system of the Atayal, Bunun, Tao (of Orchid Island, also known as the Yami), Saisiyat, Tsou and Siraya (a Plains group from the Tainan area, which figured prominently in the 17th century Dutch colonial efforts at settlement).

In the *kawas* system, spirits can be embodied in concrete forms with specific character, location and direction. In *anito* beliefs, spirits are dispersed in all beings and nature, from where they exert an influence on a community's fortunes and social order.*

---

* *Guidebook* of the Shung Ye Museum of Formosan Aborigines.

Christian churches of various denominations dominate the skylines of today's Aboriginal villages and towns.

After a successful hunt, for example, offerings would be made to the spirit of the wild boar, sika deer or muntjac, so that the hunters might avail of its courage, speed, agility or similar qualities during their future hunts.

Exhibition at the Shung Ye Museum explaining head-hunting traditions.

Head-hunting

All Aboriginal groups except the Tao practiced head-hunting to a greater or lesser extent. Surprisingly, head-hunting seems to have derived from a similar "religious" concept, though its origins are much debated. Perhaps taking a head was symbolic of attaining adulthood, or connected with ensuring an abundant harvest.

Similar to the beliefs associated with hunting animals, it was believed that capturing a human head was a source of magical power. After acquiring a head, it was wined and dined in a ceremonial feast, before being enshrined among the clan ancestors' skulls and given ritual offerings. In this way, the hunting, fighting and running skills of the dead warrior might be accessed by the living.

Before embarking on any hunt, battle or other important event, tribespeople would consult various spirits including those of their ancestors, as well as analyzing dreams and natural omens such as the flight of "divination birds," to discern the likely outcome. This work was undertaken by shamans, most of whom were female.

For extant groups, many ceremonies revolve around the worship of ancestral spirits. Every five years, the Paiwan of southern Taiwan, for example, hold a *malevaq* (five year festival) to invite their ancestors to descend from Mt. Dawu hoping, in return, for the spirits' assistance for five good harvests.

Other rituals and customs are connected with a group's myths, such as the biennial festival of the Saisiyat people to thank an ancient negrito race for teaching them farming and culture. Such festivals have often been the occasion for recounting, sometimes in song and dance, the groups' rich oral histories. Despite attempts to make written or audiovisual records, modern pressures are once again endangering the vestiges of traditional Aboriginal cultures and religions.

Aboriginal shamans' tool boxes are a combination of woven bag and intricately carved box.

Ancestor Worship
— The Soul of Chinese Religion

Although generally less obvious than the raucous worship of gods, it is ancestor worship (祖先崇拜) that lies at the true heart of Chinese religious beliefs and practices.

This is founded on a two-way relationship in which descendents take care of their ancestors' material needs for food, clothing, housing, &c. in the nether *yin* world and carrying out correct ceremonies honoring them; in return they may ask these ancestral spirits for help or protection in the earthly *yang* realm.

The Reverend George Leslie MacKay, who lived in northern Taiwan for the last thirty years of the 19th century, described Chinese "heathenism" as a "poisonous mixture" of the "ethical maxims of Confucianism," the "wretched incantations of Tauism (Daoism)" and the "idolatry of Buddhism." He then observed with percipience, however, that "their real religion is the worship of their ancestors, their real idol the ancestral tablet."*

The ancestral tablet forms the focus of worship on an altar in the home.

> **Confucius says...**
>
> "In life, serve them [your parents] according to the rites; in death, bury them according to the rites, and sacrifice to them according to the rites." (II:5)

Wandering "Hungry" Ghosts

In traditional Chinese culture, it is the existence of a legal heir who carries out the correct funeral rites and acts of worship (慎終追遠) which defines an ancestor's status. Without correct sacrifices being made to

---

* G.L. MacKay, *From Far Formosa,* 1896, p. 131

keep ancestral spirits content in the nether world, they return as wandering or "hungry ghosts" (餓鬼) to haunt the living.

The death of an unmarried woman presents a particular problem, as women's spirits are only worshiped if they have married. In this case, "ghost marriages" may be held for girls who die before wedlock.

Seven *Po* and Three *Hun*

Different schools hold different theories. One commonly-held view is that each person has seven *po* (魄; *yin* souls) and three *hun* (魂; *yang* souls). One hun soul is said to remain in the earthly realm, where it needs a place of sanctuary. This is the function of the ancestral tablet found in all homes and clan temples, to which offerings of food, candles and incense are made.

Canonization of Deities

Many among the pantheon of Chinese deities are historical figures. These include Ma-zu (媽祖) the fishermen's goddess, red-faced Guan Di (關帝), Baosheng Da-di (保生大帝) and, despite his injunction that, "Sacrificing to ancestors who are not one's own is toadying..."*, Confucius.

This demonstrates the intimate relationship between ancestor worship and the worship of popular temple deities. The King of Qingshan's (青山王) story is typical. An upright public official in life, prayers to his deceased spirit seemed to be answered by good fortune, and news of his efficaciousness as a deity spread throughout Fujian Province and then further afield.

As long as this holds true, people will continue to worship at a deity's temples and cel-

Heirlessness

Various solutions are available to those failing to produce a male heir. Simplest is straightforward adoption of a son (螟蛉子), usually by a "son going across the house" (過房子), that is, adoption of one's brother's son.

Alternatively, instead of a bride marrying out, if her husband is a younger son, he may be permitted to marry into her family (入贅).

Scholars have identified the dearth of brides available for lower class men in a culture that practiced polygamy and tolerated female infanticide as a significant cause of the many rebellions that have occurred throughout China's history.

Buddhism and Christianity were, and still are, attractive to people without heirs as neither emphasizes ancestor worship.

Four characters on the left and right of this grave remind descendents to perform "correct funeral rites and due sacrifices" (慎終追遠).

---

* *Analects of Confucius* II:24

ebrate his or her birthday. Others disappear as quickly as they appear.

G.L. MacKay recounts an interesting story of one who failed to make the grade. In 1878, a girl living near Danshui died of consumption. Proclaimed the "Virgin Goddess," her wasted body was soaked in salt and exhibited at a temple built for her. Visitors were many and their presents abundant. Nevertheless, "devotees were disappointed, for the divining-blocks gave no certain answers." He concluded that, while people might be patient with an established figure, "they had not the same respect for a new candidate." *

Passing public examination and obtaining official position brought honor on seven generations of ancestors.

Ancestral Tablets

The focus of ancestral worship is usually the spirit tablet (祖先牌位) located on the family altar in the home or local clan shrine. It is usually a small piece of wood inscribed with the name or names of family ancestors.

According to the *Records of the Historian* (史記) written by Si-ma Qian (司馬遷) during the Former Han dynasty, wooden ancestral tablets date back to the beginning of the Zhou dynasty when King Wu (武王) made a tablet for his father King Wen (文王) to take on his military campaign against Zhou (紂), the "tyrannical" last king of the Shang dynasty.

Popular mythology dates their introduction to Ding Lan (丁蘭; one of the twenty-four filial exemplars) of the Han dynasty, who carved wooden statues of his parents so that he could continue to worship them after their deaths.

"Dotting the *zhu*" Ceremony (點主禮)

It is not sufficient merely to add the name of a newly deceased family member to the family's tablet. Correct ritual must be followed. This includes a ceremony of "exorcising the spirit and dotting the *zhu*" (除靈點主), or simply "completing the *zhu* ceremony" (成主大典).

Firstly, a temporary paper tablet is set up while the wooden tablet is prepared bearing the deceased's name and a conventional funerary inscription which ends with the expression *shen zhu* (神主; another name for spirit tablets). For the time being, however, this is written as *shen wang* (神王). The final dot should be added to complete the word *zhu* by someone well-acquainted with the deceased and of upright character, while facing east, holding his breath and concentrating on a mental image of the dead person.

* G.L. MacKay, *From Far Formosa*, 1896, (p. 127)

Nature Worship

Worshiping nature (自然) and the consequent worship of heaven (敬天) are a second major theme in Chinese popular religious belief and practice, along with ancestor worship, to which they are also intimately bound.

It is thought that ancient Chinese religion probably began with a greater emphasis on nature worship aimed at procuring the rain and sunshine important to agricultural communities. Diversification led to a wide range of deities representing meteorological phenomena such as thunder and wind, and astronomical bodies, as well as the spirits of topographical features such as rivers and mountains.

Arrangement of these into a celestial administration similar to that of the emperor on earth resulted in the worship of heaven and its supreme ruler. Worship of nature, that is, respect for its unlimited power and an attempt to act in accordance with them, became encapsulated in the *Dao* (Way) of the Daoists, who sought harmony with nature and their own nature, and led to developments in sciences and arts (*feng-shui,* selection of dates, kung-fu, &c.) aimed at preserving this harmony.

A stone is worshiped among various deities at this temple in Taipei.

Worship of trees and stones is rarely seen nowadays (this example is in Hong Kong).

Astronomical and meteorological phenomena have often been deified, such as this, the "Stellar Ruler of Supreme *Yin*" (moon goddess).

Nature Deities

Scientific assistance notwithstanding, Chinese also relied on traditional religious methods to beseech divine assistance.

The pantheon of nature deities includes gods of the sun, moon, numerous constellations, wind, rain, thunder and lightning. Many others originated as such before being given more fleshed-out personalities. These include the Supreme Emperor of the Dark Heaven (玄天上帝), who evolved his human form from the earlier Dark Warrior (玄武) represented by a black turtle and snake, and earlier from the northern constellation. Similarly, Kui-xing (魁星; Top-examinee Constellation) evolved into human form, in which he is often depicted kicking the Big Dipper. He came later to represent a god of examinations and, as such, is worshiped by scholars and literati.

Ruler of Heaven

Naturally, to the Chinese mind, these myriad deities had a ruler, the Jade Emperor (玉皇大帝), or simply "Lord of Heaven" (天公). Unlike other deities, who are worshiped as statues or other images, the Jade Emperor is usually represented only by a plaque bearing his name.

Some suggest that he is a rather late arrival, brought in to give Daoism a central figure similar to the Buddha in Buddhism or Confucius in Neo-Confucianism, or to reinforce the earthly emperor's role as "son of heaven." In orthodox Daoism, he is represented as the Venerable Celestial of the Primordial Beginning (元始天尊), that is, the creator of everything.

His birthday is celebrated on the 9th day of the 1st lunar month, which, in the past, was a very solemn occasion with the year's most magnificent offerings.

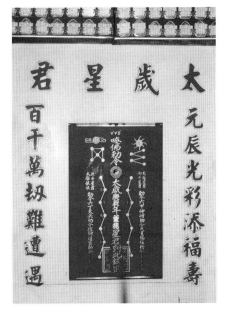

Astronomical drawings sometimes take the place of an anthropomorphic statue.

Chinese Myths—Something for Everyone

With its strong sense of continuity, veneration of ancestors, appeal to a long-gone "golden age," detailed written dynastic records and "unofficial histories" only matched in quantity by the oral traditions of the largely illiterate masses, the elevation of local heroes into deities, passionate belief in superstitions and the supernatural, as well as indistinct and fluid boundary between the human world and that of ghosts and spirits, Chinese society is perhaps the ideal fertile environment for the creation, development and preservation of religious myths and legends.

Passed from generation to generation, and retold in poetry, novels, opera, and now film and comic books, the basics of these stories blending myth, history and literary invention are known to all Chinese, while manifesting regional variations.

Some of this variation dates back to China's Neolithic period, before the Han race coalesced from different competing tribes. Thus the creation myths of China's east reflect attempts to drain marshland and cultivate rice, those of the west to control the rivers flowing from the Tibetan plateau and grow millet, while farmers on the northern plains fought an army of bears, tigers and other wild beasts.

Further variation suggests origins outside China.

Fu Xi, like other legendary figures, is usually shown unclothed in as he is said to have lived before the invention of clothing.

Legend Merges with History

The rise and fall of ancient dynasties, from the Xia (still awaiting archaeological evidence), Shang (now confirmed through the discovery of oracle bones) and Zhou, also led to fluctuations in dominance by different collections of mythology. The result is that the mythology known to today's Taipei people is a mix of overlapping, often contradictory tales. Scholarly attempts to systematize Chinese mythology are therefore doomed to failure.

Some commentators, noting the tendency for mythological heroes to be accredited with some invention or innovation, such as Fu Xi (伏羲) with fishing, Shen-Nong (神農) with agriculture, and Sui Ren (燧人) with fire, see this as the major pattern extending into historical times with the deification of Guan Di (for moral uprightness in warfare) and

Yao, Shun and the Yellow Emperor take pride of place in this temple in northern Taiwan.

Confucius (for education and statecraft).

Others, such as A.C. Graham*, see these myths being used to represent the main ideas of philosophic schools of the later Warring States period. Thus Shen-Nong (the divine farmer) represents the idealism of Lao-zi and Zhuang-zi; the Yellow Emperor (黃帝), credited with organizing the calendar, dividing lands and instituting statecraft, represents the Legalist School; Great Yu (大禹), who controlled the floodwaters, represents the utilitarianism of the Mohists (墨家); and Yao (堯) and Shun (舜), who ruled by moral influence and abdicated in favor of better men, represent Confucianism.

E.T.C. Werner[+] in *Myths and Legends of China* takes an almost opposite viewpoint, crediting the even later religious movements of Buddhism and religious Daoism with creating myths to supplement the "chilly growth of Confucian classicism."

Legendary Rebels

Joseph Needham[++] mentions another interesting group, the "legendary rebels." These include figures such as Chi You (蚩尤), legendary inventor of metallurgy; the monster Huan Dou (驩兜); Gun (鯀), who invented embankments and walls but

The legendary Emperor Shun, as described in the first of the *Twenty-Four Exemplars of Filial Piety*, was assisted in his work by elephants and birds (grave decoration).

---

* A.C. Graham, *Disputers of the Tao,* 1989, Open Court, p65 and p374.

+ E.T.C. Werner, *Myths and Legends of China,* 1922, George G. Harrap & Co.

++ Joseph Needham, *Science and Civilisation in China,* Vol II, p115.

女媧娘娘
煉石補天

Nü Wa is shown repairing heaven in this temple mural.

failed to stem floods (a project completed by his son, the Great Yu); Gong Gong (共工) chief of artisans; the Nine Li tribes (九黎) and Three Miao tribes (三苗).

Needham speculates that these were symbols of pre-feudal collectivist society (共工, for example, means "communal labor"), which resisted transformation into a feudal class-differentiated society. The Li and Miao tribes represent metalworking confraternities. These various groups are described as "disturbers of time and calendar," and as being killed (Chi You), banished (Huan Dou), executed and cut into pieces (Gun) or overcome (the Nine Li) by the Yellow Emperor in his pursuit of an organized state.

Pan Gu and the Creation of the World

Chinese cosmology has a fondness for symmetry. Thus, the imperial court and government bodies of the human world are mirrored by that of the Jade Emperor, Lord of Heaven.

The human body is similarly likened to these heavenly and earthly realms. The head is round like heaven; together the feet are flat and square like the earth. The "five viscera" (五臟): heart, liver, spleen, lungs and kidneys, are correlated with the five elements fire, wood, earth, metal, and water as well as being considered as the body's Ministries of Intelligence (while the brain was a reservoir of *yin*), Generalissimo, Storing Up, Transmission, and Ingenuity and Power.*

The Chinese "Big Bang"

This kind of cosmology also explains the origin of the world, universe and everything else.

In the time before heaven and earth had been separated, the universe was chaos "like a chicken's egg." Within this egg, Pan Gu (盤古), the first ancestor of all human beings, slept as he matured for 18,000 years. Waking, he could not see nor breathe properly. According to later popularizations of the story, groping around, he found an ax with which he struck out wildly, causing the heavens to collapse and the earth to split, as the great egg broke apart.

Light things rose upwards, becoming Heaven; heavy things sank downwards to become Earth. Heaven and Earth separated at one *zhang* (丈; about ten feet) per day, with Pan Gu growing at the same rate filling the space between. After his death, his head and four limbs became the five sacred mountains; his eyes became the sun and moon; his fatty tissues became the rivers and oceans; his veins and arteries became the roads; his flesh became the soil; his body-hair and beard became the grasses and trees; his teeth and bones became the metals and rocks; his sweat became the rain; and the insects creeping over his body became human beings.

Surprisingly, this myth is far from ancient, dating from the 4th century CE after long speculation about the world's origins. As scholars point out, the name Pan Gu may simply mean "investigating antiquity" or even just "chaotic antiquity."

---

* C.A.S. Williams, *Outlines of Chinese Symbolism & Art Motives*, Kelly and Walsh, 1932, p271.

Fu Xi and Nü Wa — Creators of People and Culture

Although only mentioned modestly in the early Zhou legends, stories surrounding Fu Xi and his sister/wife/successor Nü Wa (女媧) gained in color and complexity in later times, starting with the *Book of Changes*.

As noted in the introduction, Fu Xi (trad. 2953-2838 BCE) was credited with various innovations, including discovering the Eight Trigrams (八卦) on which the *Yi-Jing* is based. He is also said to have taught people to farm, fish and hunt with nets, and initiated the concept of marriage.

As there were no other people and after divining heaven's will, some legends recount that he married his sister, Nü Wa. Both are portrayed with human heads but snake bodies.

Nü Wa, who also appears in some lists of the Three August Ones (三皇), is said to have fashioned humankind from clay. Finding it too slow to make people one at a time, she later drew a cord through the clay so that each droplet that adhered became a human being. This is said to explain people's variation in size and ability, and the apparent inequalities of life.

Fu Xi and Nü Wa are sometimes cited as the Chinese Adam and Eve. More accurately perhaps, they represent the fundamental principles of *yin* and *yang*.

Pan Gu, creator of the world, as depicted in the Pan Gu temple in Hsin-tien (新店).

Shen-Nong — The Divine Farmer

During the "seventeen generations he ruled the world," Shen-Nong is credited with inventing the plow and developing agriculture. From nature, he gained knowledge of opposing principles and of the virtues of herbs, from which he founded herbal medicine.

Much of Shen-Nong's mythology dates from the period of proto-Daoism, which idealized the utopia of small communities living according to his "teachings." Laws, rewards and punishments are said to have been unnecessary, as people did no wrong. While the book that bears his name has been lost, many quotations survive elsewhere, exhorting rulers to plow and weave alongside the common people. Chinese emperors plowing a ritual furrow on New Year's Day may have originated from this ideal.

Sui Ren — Inventor of Fire

Sometimes placed before Fu Xi, the third August One is usually Sui Ren, discoverer or inventor of fire. Hitherto, people had eaten uncooked food, to the "detriment of their stomachs."

In later times, he was replaced as inventor of fire by Zhu Rong (祝融), a minister under the Yellow Emperor or son of his successor, Zhuan-xu (顓頊). Zhu Rong is said to both cause and prevent conflagrations and, in the latter role, receives people's offerings and prayers. He is often portrayed as an animal with a fierce red human face, whose third eye enables him to see in all directions.

Sui Ren inventing fire, as portrayed on an ROC postage stamp.

Huang Di — The Yellow Emperor

First of the Five Sovereigns is Huang Di (Yellow Emperor), whose birth is traditionally dated to around 2689 BCE.

In addition to being accredited with a number of inventions overlapping those of the Three August Ones, he is better-known for bringing to an end the "golden age of Shen-Nong" by organizing a calendar, dividing lands between feudal chiefs, and instituting statecraft and warfare.

He is supposed to have had some twenty-five sons, from whom at least twelve feudal families of the Zhou dynasty claimed descent (as do most family trees today). This meant that sacrifices to Huang Di as an ancestor were not confined to the royal house but would have been widespread in leading families throughout the nation.

He is also said to have extended China's boundaries, bringing "barbarians from beyond the four frontiers" to allegiance, a process Chinese emperors continued for the next four millennia.

Patron Deities

For reasons obvious or forgotten, various "patron deities" have become associated with particular trades or social groups. These few examples illustrate the general situation.

Carpentry

Lu Ban (魯班), a famous 6th-century-BCE mechanic from the State of Lu (魯), is said to have built a wooden falcon that could fly. He is worshiped by carpenters, joiners, blacksmiths and potters. His two wives, one with a red face, the other black, are the patronesses of lacquer-makers (red and black lacquer).

Porcelain

The pottery-making profession has always been precarious. One imperial porcelain maker is said to have been so exasperated at being unable to meet the emperor's high demands that he threw himself into the flames of his own furnace. On opening the kiln, his workers found perfect results and, greatly satisfied, the emperor honored him with deification as the god of porcelain.

Winemaking

Some four thousand years ago, Yi Di (儀狄), the inventor of winemaking, collapsed near the village of Maotai in southwest China. As a reward for rescuing her, she taught Mr. Li, a resident of the village, how to ferment rice wine.

Weaving

Old Woman Huang Dao (黃道婆), who lived in the 14th century, is said to have invented the flocking-bow and the loom, and to have taught people the arts of spinning and weaving. For this, her statue is worshiped as the goddess of weaving.

Flowers

Hua Xian (花仙; flower immortal) is the popular goddess of flowers. She is accompanied by two attendants carrying baskets of flowers.

Brush-making

Meng Tian (蒙恬), who died in 209 BCE (ironically, just after the Qin emperor had burnt all of China's books except a few on farming and warfare) is credited with introducing the Chinese brush-

pen, for which he is honored by today's brush-makers.

Horse King and Ox King

King of Horses (馬王), an ugly ogre with three eyes and four hands is worshiped by horse-rearers and rural communities. The King of Oxen (牛王) is prayed to by cattle farmers. Both are said to protect the animals from evil spirits and disease.

Kitchen God

Worshiped on his birthday at the beginning of the eighth lunar month by cooks and kitchen workers, the God of the Stove (灶神) is honored by everyone on the 23rd day of the 12th month.

...and Many More

Among the Eight Immortals Lü Dong-bin (呂洞賓) is patron deity of barbers, Cao Guo-jiu (曹國舅) of actors, and Lan Cai-he (藍采和) of minstrels;

Ma-tou Niang (馬頭娘; horse-headed woman) is worshiped by growers of mulberry trees and silk workers;

Cai Lun (蔡倫) is honored for inventing paper; cobblers worship Sun Bin (孫臏).

Story-tellers honor Cang Jie (倉頡), the legendary inventor of writing;

prostitutes worship Guanyin (觀音) or Zhu Ba-jie (豬八戒), the pig in *Journey to the West* (西遊記) because "all men behave like pigs";

thieves often honor Song Jiang (宋江) who fermented rebellion in the 12th century and is immortalized in the novel *The Water Margin* (水滸傳);

and butchers worship Fan Kuai (樊噲) or Zhang Fei (張飛), who made his living selling pork until swearing brotherhood with Guan Yu (關羽) and Liu Bei (劉備) as recorded in the *Romance of the Three Kingdoms* (三國演義).

1. King of Horses (temple statue).
2. Cang Jie inventing writing (postage stamp).
3. "Pigsy" (temple statue).
4. Zhang Fei (temple mural).

Immortality

Traditional Chinese culture places the world of the dead firmly inside the known universe. There is no clear division between this life and the afterlife, therefore, as rather than being dichotomous these were considered as merely different stages within a single continuum. The dissipation of a person's "three superior *hun* (魂; *yang* souls) and seven *po* (魄; *yin* souls)" at death would also necessitate that any search for immortality would tend to be material.*

Eternal Search for Immortality

Although the search for physical immortality predated religious Daoism, it became a dominant concern within Daoist practice. (Interestingly, although absent from Buddhism, which teaches that death is followed by rebirth, poor translations and reliance on Daoist terminology meant that Nirvana was misunderstood initially as a kind of immortality. Buddhism was seen as simply another Daoist sect and had to wait for increased contact with India and more accurate explanations of its concepts before it could be established as a separate religion.)

It is ironic, therefore, that Daoism, which is often seen as inhabiting the spiritual end of the spectrum of Chinese thought, should have expended so much effort on attaining something as material as "long life and immortality" (長生不死).

This is in stark contrast to the attitude shown towards death in the "philosophic Daoist" texts on which "religious Daoism" claims to be based. Zhuang-zi, for example, expresses an ecstatic tone when he writes about death, is supposed to have played music on a pot at the death of his wife, and mocks the rites of mourning.

Other passages can be interpreted as suggesting that following the "Way," that is, living in harmony with one's true nature, nurturing one's

> **Zhuang-zi says,**
>
> "Death and life are destined; that they have the constancy of morning and evening."[+]

qi (氣; vital energy), and thus returning to a primordial wholeness, did raise the possibility of immortality.

> **Zhuang-zi also says,**
>
> "In the mountains of far-off Ku-yi there lives a daemonic man (神人), whose skin and flesh are like ice and snow, who is gentle as a virgin. He does not eat the five grains but sucks in the wind and drinks the dew; he rides the vapour of the clouds, yokes flying dragons to his chariot, and roams beyond the four seas."[++]

---

* Science and Civilisation in China; Joseph Needham; Cambridge University Press; Vol. 2.

+ Chuang Tzu - The Inner Chapters; A.C. Graham; George Allen & Unwin; 1981; p86.

++ Chuang Tzu - The Inner Chapters; A.C. Graham; George Allen & Unwin; 1981; p46

Similar interpretations are made about passages in the *Classic of Virtue and its Way* (道德經; *Dao-de Jing*), the short but highly influential book probably dating from the late 4th or early 3rd century BCE but attributed to the mythical 6th century BCE figure Lao-zi.

> **Lao-zi says,**
>
> "In concentrating your *qi* can you become as supple as a babe."

Paradox

This led to a paradox within Daoist teachings, for while esoteric methods designed to attain immortality for a successful few were also said to increase longevity in the many, Daoism also taught that one's lifespan was ultimately predestined and beyond human intervention.

Nevertheless, over many centuries, "gentlemen of occult arts" (方士), developed a wide range of techniques aimed at "returning to the source of existence," being at one with the Dao, and attaining longevity and immortality.

These included dietary practices, moral behavior, meditation, breathing techniques, sexual practices, physical exercises and yogic techniques (which led to today's well-known martial arts of Tai-chi and Kung-fu), medical practices, "interior alchemy" (內丹; *nei-dan*) and "exterior alchemy" (外丹; *wai-dan*).

Like alchemists worldwide, Daoist practitioners of *wai-dan* sought the elixir of life, a pill created through the transformation of chemical substances that could change the transitory material of the body into indestructible matter. Since, for the Chinese, immortality is the attainment of human perfection and gold is the perfection of metals, most alchemical compounds involved swallowing gold, jade (thought to dispel evil) or cinnabar (丹; *dan*), which was supposed to have magical properties.

Alchemists sought to purify cinnabar (a sulfide of mercury, which, therefore, is more likely to shorten life expectancy), reasoning the purer it is the quicker one's attainment of immortality. As Ge Hong (葛洪), China's most famous Daoist alchemist, wrote in *Embracer of the Unhewn Block* (抱朴子), "If a person ingests once-transformed cinnabar, it will take him three years to become an immortal..." but only "three days if consuming nine-times transformed cinnabar."

Fields of Worms

Inner alchemy is concerned with taming the thought processes and purifying the three life-preserving energies of "essence" (精), "vital energy" (氣) and "spirit" (神). Using a language similar to that of external alchemy, the body is compared to the alchemist's melting pot. Of particular importance are the three "cinnabar fields" (丹田) where *qi* energy concentrates: the brain, near the heart, and below the navel. Each field is said to be inhabited by its own deity and, for some schools, by its own "harmful worm" (三蟲).

Destruction of these "three worms" is the preparatory phase of attaining immortality. One method started with abstinence from cereals, then progressed to exclusion of wine, meat and plants with strong flavors such as onions and garlic.

Most schools also favored some kind of esoteric sexual practice called "techniques of the bed-chamber" (房中之法) that had originally developed independently of Daoism. These included union of male and female in the "way of nourishing life by means of *yin* and *yang*" (陰陽養生之道) and "refraining from ejaculation" (還精補腦), as it was believed that semen retention could prolong life and improve the intellect. According to popular myth, sexual regulation was supposed to have been practiced by Lao-zi himself. By the Ming dynasty, however, such practices had been driven underground and only found in secret sects emphasizing sexual routes to immortality.

Becoming an Immortal

Not surprisingly, cynics pointed out that even those who practiced these techniques for decades and led upright moral lives still met with eventual death. This was explained as a "false death" and that, although those who attained immortality were given normal funeral rites, what was placed in the coffin was not a corpse but a sword or bamboo stick.

Daoist schools kept detailed records of those supposed to have become an immortal (仙). Many such figures achieved legendary status, the best known group is the Eight Immortals (八仙), indeed, they are among the best-recognized figures in the entire body of Chinese mythology.

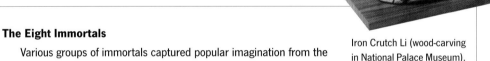

Iron Crutch Li (wood-carving in National Palace Museum).

The Eight Immortals

Various groups of immortals captured popular imagination from the Tang dynasty onwards and, by the Ming dynasty, the following eight had assumed center stage, appearing in mythological tales as well as religious and secular art.

1. Iron Crutch Li (李鐵拐), easily recognized by his disabled body propped against his "iron crutch," is probably best known of the eight. Leaving his body under the supervision of a pupil for seven days, his soul departed but, upon return, found the student had burnt his body because his mother was critically ill and he went home. Looking around for a corpse to borrow, the first Li found was that of a crippled beggar with blackened face.

He is usually depicted carrying a gourd containing magic potions, often accompanied by a bat.

Some accredit Lao-zi with teaching him the immortals' arts; others say it was Queen Mother of the West (西王母).

2. Lü Dong-bin (呂洞賓) often portrayed as leader of the Eight Immortals, he is also accredited with teaching magic arts to several of them. Perhaps a historical figure from Tang dynasty northern China or the Song dynasty, Lü is said to have adapted the ideas of "external alchemy" into the techniques of "internal alchemy," thereby developing a new pathway to immortality.

One tale tells of Lü drinking in a wine shop and, instead of paying, he painted two cranes on the wall. These became famous and attracted many customers. When Lü's debt had been discharged, the cranes flew away.

His symbol is a magic sword with which he slays demons.

3. Zhang Guo-lao (張國老) was perhaps a Daoist from Tang dynasty Shanxi Province (山西). He is said to have a white donkey capable of traveling a thousand *li* (c. 500 km) a day but which could be folded into his pocket like a piece of paper. Another myth says he was originally a woodcutter, and yet another that he was a bat, which transformed into a man.

His symbols are his donkey, a long bamboo cane and a "fish-drum."

4. He Xian-gu (何仙姑) is the only female member of the Eight Immortals. She is said to have gained the ability of flight as a child and also vowed not to marry. She was attacked by a demon and rescued by Lü Dong-bin who initiated her into the group.

Her symbol is a lotus (荷 also pronounced he).

5. Cao Guo-jiu (曹國舅) was perhaps brother-in-law or uncle of a Song dynasty emperor, who withdrew to the mountains after a brother committed murder but, in any case, "since childhood he had loved the secret Way of things."

He is usually depicted holding his symbol, a pair of castanets.

6. Lan Cai-he (藍采和) is sometimes portrayed as a man, sometimes as a woman, and occasionally as a hermaphrodite. He started life as a beggar, drunk or street singer, who, one day,

Detail from an Eight Immortals cloth.

disrobed, mounted a crane and disappeared into the clouds.

His symbol is a bowl of flowers or fruit, or sometimes a flute.

7. Han Xiang-zi (韓湘子) is the most historically substantiated of the Eight Immortals, being the nephew of the famous Tang dynasty statesman and man of letters Han Yu (韓愈; 768-824).

He is said to have caused peonies to blossom in winter, on whose petals appeared a poem, stating,

"Clouds veil the peaks of Jin-ling Mountain.

Where is your home?

Deep lies the snow on Lan Pass

and the horses will go no further."

Later, Han Yu fell from imperial favor and was banished. On reaching Lan Pass, the snow was so deep he could advance no further. Han Xiang-zi suddenly appeared and cleared the snow, making another prophecy that his uncle would be forgiven and regain his official position. This soon came true.

Han is identified by a flute, a bunch of flowers or peach.

8. Zhong Li-quan (鍾離權) perhaps dates from the Han or Song dynasty, for whom he fought as a senior officer, after which he retired to the mountains to pursue immortality through alchemical means.

He is portrayed as bald figure with a long beard and large, bare stomach. His symbol is a fan, which he uses to bring people back to life.

The most common depictions of the Eight Immortals as a group are in "The Eight Immortals Cross the Ocean" (八仙過海) in which each displays his talents, and Eight Immortals Celebrate a Birthday (八仙慶壽), when they gather at the invitation of the Queen Mother of the West.

Queen Mother of the West

Two other deities who are closely connected to the ideas and practices of immortality are Chang-E (嫦娥) and Queen Mother of the West (西王母).

The latter seems to have started her mythological career as a human-faced monster with a leopard's tale and tiger's roar who lived in a cave, ate people and spread epidemics.

By around two thousand years ago, she had become a beautiful goddess who protected against epidemics, and lived in a white jade tower on the Kunlun Mountains (崑崙山) somewhere to the west of China.

Every three thousand years, her peach tree of immortality flowers and produces one fruit, at which time she invites all immortals and deities to partake in a feast including this peach. As such, she is accorded the status of chief of all immortals.

She is prayed to in times of epidemics, worshiped for those seeking immortality, and given birthday celebrations on the 3rd day of the 3rd lunar month.

Chang-E ascending to the moon after eating the drug of immortality.

Artistic Symbolism

Statues, pictures and embroidery often contain symbols alluding to longevity and immortality. In addition to the individual symbols of the Eight Immortals, most of these are animals thought to live to very old ages, such as turtles, cranes and deer; or plants that are hardy such as pine and bamboo, plum and, above all, the peach.

God(s) of Wealth

Walk into any provisions store in any China Town around the world, from Vancouver to Jakarta, and you can buy a small statue of the "god of wealth" (財神) to furnish your home altar or complete your *feng-shui* preparations, though do not try to buy the proprietor's own statue.

There are, in fact, various gods of wealth, as well as wealth-beckoning cats, and numerous other deities to whom people pray for financial assistance.

Civil and Military Wealth

One major division is between "civil" (文) and "martial" (武) gods of wealth.

The latter is usually represented by the red-faced Guan Yu, while the most popular civil god of wealth is the "Stellar Gentleman who Increases Wealth" (增福財帛星君), the celes-

Civil gods of wealth (temple statues).

Fu (happiness), Lu (prosperity through official rank) and Shou (longevity) in a grave decoration.

Military gods of wealth (temple statues).

A god of wealth takes part in all temple activities to ensure a community's continued prosperity.

tial part of his title derives from a legend connecting him with one of the seven stars of the Big Dipper and, therefore, with the northerly direction.

The God of Increasing Wealth is portrayed as an elegant scholar with a white face and long beard. In his left hand he holds a jade *ru-yi* (如意) scepter, in his right hand a treasure bowl on which is written "Beckoning wealth—bringing treasure" (招財進寶). He is often shown together with the trinity of Fu (福; happiness), Lu (祿; prosperity through official rank) and Shou (壽; longevity), and a rarer figure, Xi-shen (喜神; a god of pleasure or love). Together, these represent the Five Blessings that go to make up a happy life.

The God of Wealth acts as chief minister in a celestial Ministry of Wealth. His officials include the Celestial Venerable who Brings Treasures (招寶天尊), Celestial Venerable who Presents Jewels (納珍天尊), Immortal Official of Commercial Profit (利市仙官) and so forth, though there is great regional variation, and many deities are worshiped as gods of wealth in their own right.

Other "folk figures" include the Wealth-Beckoning Child (招財童子), Cash Tree with coin leaves and ingot fruit, God of Wealth of the Five Roads (五路財神) worshiped by innkeepers, and Lord of the Land (土地公), who is then portrayed holding ingots or coins.

Shou (longevity) decorating a vase used for temple flowers.

Heartless Entrepreneurs

One legend traces the god of wealth back to Bi Gan (比干),a minister under the 11th century tyrant king Zhou (紂), last ruler of the Shang dynasty. Zhou cut out Bi's heart to see if a sage really did have seven cavities as rumored.

He was later enfeoffed as one of the seven stars of the Big Dipper and subsequently became worshiped as the God of Wealth.

God of Wealth (bas-relief temple decoration).

"Wealth-Beckoning Cats"

Found next to most cash registers throughout Taipei, Wealth-Beckoning Cats (招財貓) are one legacy of Taiwan's fifty years of Japanese rule (1895-1945).

Known as *maneki-neko* in Japanese, they are mostly yellow (money-making) or white (lucky), though black-colored (warding off evil) cats also exist.

There are various legends regarding the cats' origins, most dating from the Edo period (1603-1867).

Grateful Geisha

Usugumo, a prostitute, was inseparable from her cat Tama (玉; jade). It even accompanied her to the bathroom. Some jealous people hinted she was under the cat's spell, so the brothel owner killed Tama, only to find a snake's head in its mouth. Usugumo erected a tomb to Tama, whose popularity spread.

Appreciative Abbot

Returning from a hunting trip, Edo Mayor Ii Nataka was enticed inside the Gootoku Temple by a cat. Saved a soaking from an unexpected thunderstorm, he credited the cat and patronized the temple, whose abbot commissioned a statue to his "luck-bringing cat."

Fortunate Fishmonger

Tama belonged to an Edo moneylender, whose client, a fishmonger, gave him fish. After pawning all his furniture, the fishmonger found two gold coins under his pillow, which he attributed to Tama.

Lucky Lady

A cat appeared in a destitute woman's dreams, instructing her to make a statue of the cat. Placing it on the "god shelf" in her home, she made offerings and good fortune followed. She later started a business selling ceramic cat statues and made a fortune.

Repentant Rake

A younger son of a prominent Edo family almost brought his family to ruin through gambling, only to be saved by his cat, Tama, who appeared holding a gold coin. Each time he lost that money, he asked Tama to find a coin, which it did but seemed to become thinner. The man followed his cat, and saw it pray at a temple, "Take of my paws, take of my feet, give me a gold coin..." as it became fainter until it finally disappeared. The gambler reformed his ways, restored his family fortunes, and, with a statue of Tama to welcome customers and remind him of his past, started the tradition of wealth-beckoning cats.

This last version is the best-known in Taiwan.

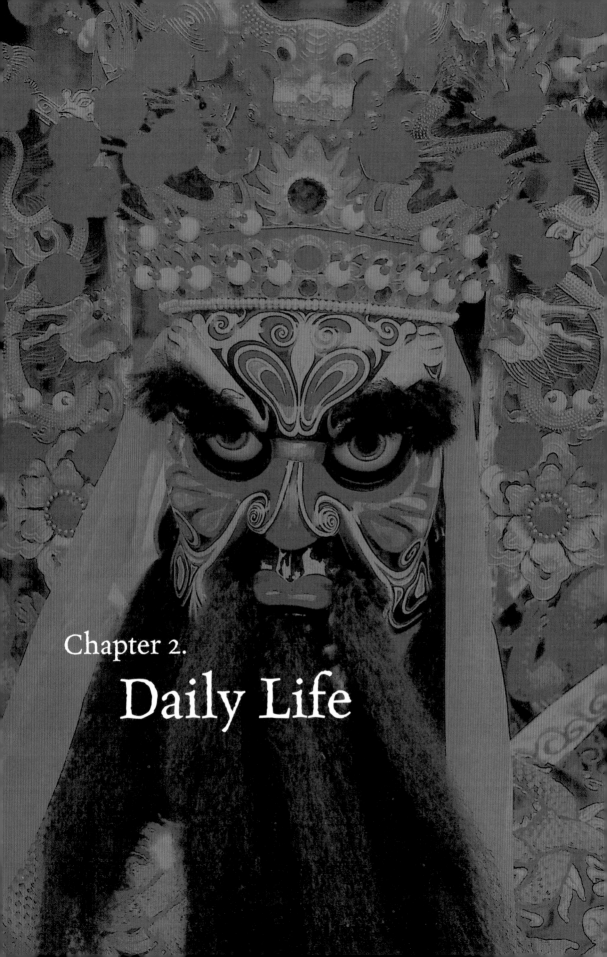

Chapter 2.
Daily Life

Worship, Prayer and Offerings

Despite the existence of priestly authority, orthodox scriptures and prescribed rituals, religion in Taipei is primarily about practice, about a personal relationship with deities and spirits, about harnessing the powers of the spirit world to help people in the human realm.

While the ceremonies and festivals that punctuate the year are important and conspicuous, a person's relationship with ancestral spirits and tutelary deities is established on the daily practices of veneration, worship, prayer and offerings. Although such practices and beliefs vary from person to person, there are a number of common themes to the *bai-bai* (拜拜; worship) practices of Taipei citizens today.

Deities or ancestors are consulted at all important stages of life.

Food, incense and joss money appear on most offering tables (the food may not be eaten until the spirits have satisfied their hunger).

1. Expression of Respect (敬意)

The first thing a believer does before addressing a deity or ancestral spirit is to adopt a respectful attitude (changing clothes and washing oneself if necessary), in order to approach the temple altar or tablets and statues in the

Incense

The Chinese word for incense, *xiang* (香) means "fragrance," which is produced by burning the resins, barks, woods, dried flowers, fruit and seeds of various botanical species. The main ingredient of Taiwanese incense is sandalwood (檀), which comes from the Southeast Asian *Santalum album* tree.

Since prehistoric times, smoke rising from incense has symbolized a believer's prayers floating upwards towards the heavens. (An alternative theory suggests that burning incense derives from ancient animal sacrifices.) The fragrant smell also symbolizes the pure thoughts in a supplicant's heart.

Buddhist incense traditionally has five ingredients: sandalwood, aloeswood, cloves, saffron and camphor.

In Taipei's temples, incense forms an integral part of most public ceremonies and private rituals (though the government is now investigating possible incense-related cancers among priests and regular temple-goers).

Ash from burnt incense is believed to have magical powers and is sometimes consumed as a spiritual medicine. Incense ash is also placed in pendants as a talisman and worn around the neck when traveling far from home.

When Chinese immigrants first arrived in Taiwan, they brought incense from the censers of their home temples. Similarly, when a son leaves his parental home, he takes incense from in front of the ancestral tablet.

Shopkeepers and farmers burn large quantities of joss money on the *ya* offerings twice a month.

home in a tranquil manner. In an act known as "new tea" (新茶), offerings such as tea or wine and food are refreshed. Candles (now often electric lamps) and incense are lit, and, when appropriate and where convenient, "gold paper" (金紙) joss money is burnt. The supplicant then puts his or her hands together before the chest, and bows towards the deities.

He or she is now ready to communicate any thoughts, feelings or requests.

2. Thanksgiving (謝恩)

Thanking deities for help received in response to earlier entreaties is one frequent theme of Taiwanese *bai-bai*. Similarly, prayers are offered after recovering from illness, or simply for some perceived good fortune. The

A respectful attitude is exhibited by lighting candles.

Continuous burning of incense fills temples with fragrant smells (but, perhaps, also with carcinogenic chemicals).

first and second of these are often connected with the realization of a pledge undertaken by the believer, the only difference being that the offerings should be greater in quantity than when beseeching divine assistance. For example, if three kinds of meat are offered at the pledge, five kinds should be presented as an indication of the "profit" attained through the deity's intervention. Such "profit" may be financial gain, promotion, marriage, childbirth &c.

A Daoist priest is often engaged to perform a ceremony on behalf of the supplicant. Alternatively, this form of worship can be seen during marriage rituals or on the birthdays of family elders.

3. Offering Apology (謝罪)

If, instead of being blessed by good fortune, one's life or those of one's family seem to be

Temples are provided with large tables for offerings to host deities.

dogged by ill health or bad luck, people of religious conviction assume that they have offended a malicious spirit or demon. Although similar in appearance to thanksgiving (offerings, incense, etc.), the thoughts behind them are entirely different.

Divination may be used to ascertain the nature of the offense and the deity offended. *Bwa-bwey*, the throwing of divinatory blocks (筊杯) providing yes/no answers to questions asked by the diviners, is one common method.

4. Preventing Haunting (避祟)

Since it is believed that each piece of ground and each building has its own specific spirits, many possibly uncared for by descendents and therefore liable to malicious acts, care must be taken to avoid causing offense.

In particular, whenever erecting a building, changing use of a building, clearing land, preparing a gravesite or making changes to one, or when choosing a location for some specific use, care should be taken to select auspicious dates and to follow the advice of a *feng-shui* expert. Offerings are also made in ritual manner.

Buddhist Worship

Whenever Buddhist disciples enter a room containing a statue of the Buddha or senior monastic, they bow and prostrate themselves three times in a reverential manner.

This should not be confused with the worship of deities and spirits. It is merely showing respect for one's teacher, the Buddha, represented by the statue, monk or nun.

A Buddhist nun bows and kneels before a statue of the historic Buddha as a mark of respect for her teacher. Finally, opening her palms (and heart), she is ready to receive his teachings.

Rituals, Pledges and Health
—The Taiwanese Take on Vegetarianism

One of Taipei's more surprising statistics is that there are almost two hundred vegetarian restaurants within the city boundaries. Unlike in the West, vegetarianism is not generally promoted on grounds of animal welfare or even human health, but is most often a personal matter that Taiwanese do not feel motivated to discuss.

This is because vegetarianism is predominantly a religious concern and, among the Chinese "three religions," is predominantly a Buddhist concern.

In keeping with the first precept, a Buddhist nun fills up on vegetarian fare.

Moreover, vegetarian restaurants' customers are mostly part-time practitioners, who refrain from meat only on religious holidays, at funerals, before a trip to the temple, or for a limited period as a pledge (許願) or fulfillment of a pledge (還願). Pledges are made in the hope of securing spiritual help in business or examinations, or for one's health or that of a relative.

The most common days for religious vegetarian observance (like many religious activities), are the first and fifteenth days of each lunar month.

The Five Precepts

1. Do not destroy life (不殺生).
2. Do not steal (不偷盜).
3. Do not commit adultery (不淫慾).
4. Do not speak falsely (不妄語).
5. Do not drink liquor (不飲酒).

There are further sets:

1. Eight for the layperson (adding: no food after midday; no garlands or perfume; and chastity).
2. Ten precepts for the novice monastic (adding: no singing or theater; and no acquisition of valuable metal or jewels).
3. 250 for monks.
4. 350 for nuns;
   and others.

Buddhist Doctrine

Taiwanese monastic and lay Buddhists accept at least five precepts (五戒).

In Taiwan, the first of these, "do not destroy life," is taken as referring to all "sentient beings" and, therefore, as an injunction not to eat meat.

Buddhist traditions differ, however. The Dalai Lama, for example, eats meat every second day but, like most of us, has other people kill animals for him. Japanese monks of the Pureland School (淨土宗) may eat meat, drink alcohol and marry.

Vegetarianism was not part of the earliest Buddhist tradition. The historical Buddha is said to have eaten whatever he was given in public alms, and is recorded as recommending certain meat dishes to his disciples. Before attaining enlightenment, Siddhartha Gautama experimented with various diets including vegetarianism, but abandoned them believing that they did not contribute to spiritual development. This is part of the Middle Way (中道) advocated in the later period of his teaching. (Some accounts suggest that the Buddha even died after eating bad meat, while others say that there was a considerable time gap in between.)

Other Regulations

Other Buddhist dietary regulations for monks and nuns generally include eating only once per day (nothing after midday), being dependent on the local community for food through begging, and not eating ten specific kinds of meat, for example, the flesh of elephants, tigers and snakes.

For social as well as doctrinal reasons, these rules are not practiced widely in Taiwan. However, there is one further dietary prohibition which, to the consternation of many Western vegetarians living in Taipei, means that local meat-free restaurants are also garlic and onion-free.

A vegetarian diet is becoming even healthier as organic produce grows in popularity.

The swastika is often a sign for vegetarian food (素食).

This is because the *Surangama sutra* (楞嚴經), an 8th century Mahayana text, says, "All living creatures seeking enlightenment should refrain from the five pungent vegetables of this world. If eaten cooked, these five pungent foods will arouse lust; if eaten raw, will increase anger." It also explains that, when reading the sutras, the breath of someone who has consumed these vegetables will drive away good spirits.

These "five pungent vegetables" (五辛 or 五葷) are garlic, leeks, and three kinds of onions.

The Language of Vegetarianism

"I am vegetarian" in Chinese is "*wo chi su*" (我吃素) and, although there is no standard expression for "vegan" (which only entered the English language in the 1940s), "*yan-shou su-shi*" (嚴守素食) "strictly-observed vegetarianism" is generally understood, as is "*chi quan- su*" (吃全素) "complete vegetarianism."

Perhaps because Taiwan's vegetarianism is closely tied to long-established Buddhist teachings, there is little interest in veganism and little debate over definitions and practices. Due to the small chance of inadvertently eating a fertilized embryo, there has been discussion regarding the consumption of eggs, however. Ironically, today's intensive farming methods mean that eggs cannot be fertilized, and so are now largely accepted by Taiwan's vegetarian community.

Signs of Vegetarianism

Vegetarian restaurants in Taipei can generally be recognized by the single character 素 pronounced *su* and meaning literally "pure, plain or simple." Perhaps even more common is the swastika 卍 (pronounced *wan*, though rarely used in spoken Chinese), which is used because of its connection with Buddhism.

卍

Buddhism adopted the swastika from the earlier Hinduism of India, which, in turn, had taken it from the pre-Aryan Mohenjo-Daro culture of the 3rd millennium BC.

It is probably older still, and is thought to have been an ancient sun symbol (the legs representing the sun's clockwise movement through the sky), or a cross, or perhaps a wheel of the sun god's chariot.

The word *swastika* means "well-being" or "benediction," deriving from the Sanskrit words *su* (well) and *asti* (the third person singular of the verb "to be").

The Buddha does an impression of the Hindu god Vishnu who is said to have an "auspicious sea cloud" breast curl in the shape of a swastika.

Occasionally in Taiwan, but very common among Overseas Chinese communities, particularly in Southeast Asia, the word 齋 (pronounced *zhai*) is used to advertise vegetarian fare.

During the 19th and early 20th centuries, religious sects known as (齋教; vegetarian religion) developed in Taiwan. Drawing on teachings from Confucianism, Daoism and particularly Buddhism, these were groups of semi-clerical semi-lay followers, who took vows of vegetarianism and conducted their own ceremonies among "vegetarian friends" (齋友) in "vegetarian assemblies" (齋會).

The opposite of 素, 卍 or 齋, that is, a sign for a non-vegetarian restaurant, is usually simply the absence of these characters. However, where vegetarian food might be expected, mixed or meat dishes are identified by the character 葷 (*hun*) which, as seen above, is possibly derived from a word for garlic and other pungent vegetables.

Illustration showing Confucius making an offering of a carp.

Other Religions and Food

Despite the dead pigs, goats, chickens, fish and whatever else to be found displayed as offerings at Daoist temples, vegetarianism as a vow or in fulfillment of a promise is just as popular among non-Buddhists.

Although Taiwan's Aborigines all reared pigs and most kept chickens, many used them for sacrifices rather than personal consumption. Even today, some Aborigines do not eat chicken or eggs for this reason.

Confucius says...

The *Analects of Confucius* (論語) mention sacrificial sheep used to keep one's ancestors informed of the New Moon (III:17 告朔之餼羊), and oxen used in the Sacrifice to the Hills and Streams. (VI:4 山川)

Birth, Marriage and Death

Part I: Conception, Pregnancy and Birth

Ancestor worship is a, perhaps the, key element of Chinese religious practice and thought. In return for protection by deceased clan ancestors, living descendents must make regular offerings and, most importantly, produce sons of their own to continue the family line.

Conception

In former times, it was desired that conception should occur as soon as possible after the bride moved to live with her husband's family.

For those having difficulty falling pregnant, a trip to the temple was a must. While sincere prayers to any deity, ancestral spirit, buddha or bodhisattva were (and still are) believed to help, and those to a female such as Mazu (媽祖) or the bodhisattva Guanyin (觀音) as being particularly efficacious, most popular are entreaties to Zhusheng Niangniang (註生娘娘).

The object of many would-be mothers, Zhusheng Niangniang (註生娘娘), the "Queen Registrar of Births."

Six of the Twelve Maternal Ancestors who assist in childbirth through the twelve months of the year.

Zhusheng Niangniang — the "Queen Registrar of Births"

If, as claimed, Zhusheng Niangniang is a historical figure dating from the Tang dynasty, her name has long been forgotten. Whether historical or otherwise, her birthday is celebrated on the 20th day of the 3rd lunar month.

She is worshiped as a subsidiary deity at many temples around Taipei, including Longshan (龍山寺) and Bao-An (保安宮) temples. The latter has an intimate side chapel dedicated to her, with large statues for on-the-spot worship and smaller ones for home loan in the most stubborn cases of difficult conception. Along both walls are statues of the Twelve Maternal Ancestors (十二婆祖), one of whom assists in childbirth through each of the twelve months.

Like Seventh Mother (七娘媽) or Madame Lin Shui (臨水夫人), the Queen Registrar of Births is said to also help as a spiritual midwife. Married women therefore pray to Zhusheng Niangniang for babies and unproblematic childbirth; unmarried ones for a suitable marriage. She is also believed to protect offspring throughout their childhoods and promote healthy development.

Her birthday celebrations include donations of floral hairpins to those followers who wish to conceive; white for those who want a boy and red for girls. People also bring baby shoes or clothes to the temple to receive the goddess' blessing.

Pregnancy

Once a woman has become pregnant, furniture should not be moved in her room, nails should not be hammered into the walls, nor should she use scissors, for fear of harming the fetus' spirit, which is believed to be present already in the room. The window should not be obscured in case the child is born blind; the mother-to-be should not attend a puppet show in case the baby has soft bones or no bones at all; and under no circumstances should she attend a funeral; indeed, it is best if she does not even catch sight of a coffin.

Even in the modern city of Taipei, many of these customs are still adhered to. Less so the traditional methods for "transforming a female fetus into a male." Firstly, it was necessary to ascertain the sex of the baby: "boys left; girls right." Only then, if necessary, a blind medium or fortune-teller would be invited into the house to pray and burn talismans. (Taiwan's present birthrate is about 110 boys for each 100 girls, suggesting that modern parents have found some alternative means to ascertain and ensure the gender of their offspring.)

If a woman gives birth to a daughter, traditional practices prescribe eating pig stomach within ten days as a means of guaranteeing a son at the next conception.

Birth

Traditionally, a boy's umbilical cord was burned and its ashes placed in a bottle with lime. It was believed that if a man in adulthood took this to a law court during litigation, he would be sure to win his case. A girl's umbilical cord was thrown into a river.

Today, a Third Morning Ceremony (三朝禮) is still held at which the baby receives a ritual bathing. Cassia flowers, tangerine leaves, longan leaves and a small stone are boiled in water, which is said to ensure the baby will himself produce many successful descendants. Joss money is burnt and offerings are made to the family's ancestors to inform them of the clan's newest arrival.

Although a baby's name must be registered within the first ten days, he or she is given a nickname during the preschool years. Boys are sometimes given female names to trick malicious spirits into overlooking a newborn heir, especially if a couple has finally produced their first child late in life, or when a boy is born after a succession of girls.

A mother-to-be offers a prayer to Zhusheng Niangniang at Taipei's Longshan Temple.

Names are not normally chosen until after birth to enable fortune-tellers to calculate the balance of the five elements (五行: metal, wood, water, fire and earth) on the basis of the Eight Characters (八字), since a suitable name may be chosen to make up the deficiency.

The baby's hair is cut on the 24th day after birth in the hope that he or she will follow the *Twenty-Four Exemplars of Filial Piety* (二十四孝).

The family genealogy (家譜) tracing back to pre-imperial or even legendary ancestors is kept up-to-date by hand until a new printing is deemed necessary.

At one year, a child participates in predicting its own destiny. (Photo by Hsu Yu-bin)

Grabbing Around

Another, somewhat less serious, activity used to determine the baby's destiny is usually performed on its first birthday, though sometimes after one hundred days. Known as "grabbing around the circle" (抓週), the infant is placed on a table and surrounded by twelve objects. Depending on which object he or, more recently, she chooses first, the child's future profession is predicted.

There are various traditions as to what items might be offered; those for a boy often include a book, pen, ink, chicken leg, piece of pork, abacus, weighing scale, coins, block of wood, onion, lump of earth and loaf of bread (those for a girl include such items as needles or kitchen utensils).

When grabbed first, these items indicate respectively a scholar, calligrapher, glutton, businessman, millionaire, carpenter, genius, farmer, baker and so forth. Oddly, onions (蔥) indicate intelligence (聰明) and therefore a genius because both include a character pronounced *cong*.

One Month Old

When the infant reaches its first full month (滿月), more offerings are made to ancestors and deities, and a party is thrown for family and friends. Good presents for friends to give the child include pieces of gold jewelry, red envelopes of cash (紅包), clothes, diapers and powdered milk. The mother's family presents the baby with a set of "head-to-tail" clothes (頭尾).

Other sets of such clothes are given after four months and one year. The maternal grandmother gives a tiger hat (小虎帽) or even a complete outfit of tiger clothes to scare away evil demons. Throughout childhood, youngsters are encouraged to wear small lockets around their necks when venturing outside. These often contain talismans or incense collected from the censer of a favored temple.

A child dressed in his tiger clothes arrives by scooter at the Longshan Temple.

During her "sitting month" (坐月子) after giving birth, a mother should neither leave home nor wash her hair. If she must go outside, an umbrella should be used to hide her from the deities' sight, and she must wear warm clothes to protect her from winds and disease so that she is in good condition to conceive again as soon as possible.

Part II: Love and Marriage

In traditional Chinese poetry, painting, customs and even laws, romantic love is recognized as one of the finest human emotions and accorded a similarly high status, so long as it did not interfere with more important social functions. Unfortunately, these include the arrangement of a suitable marriage.

Marriage was considered a contract between two families rather than individuals and was orchestrated by a professional matchmaker. Similarly, since same-gender relationships could not produce a male heir, despite a tolerance suggested in classical Chinese literature, homosexuality did not constitute reasonable grounds for refusing marriage.

The Old Man Under the Moon is said to tie people together at birth so that they eventually meet and marry.

Yuan-fen and the Old Man Under the Moon

Chinese often talk about *yuan-fen* (緣分), the fate that brings people together, lovers in particular. There is also an Old Man Under the Moon (月下老人) responsible. Checking people's names from a list provided to him by the Seventh Mother (七娘媽), he ties couples together at birth using invisible red thread. If this succeeds in drawing them towards each other innocently as life takes its course, then it should eventually result in marriage.

(One place to find the Old Man is in the far left corner at Longshan Temple (龍山寺) in Wanhua.)

Taiwan's Aboriginal groups, by comparison, seem to have practiced love marriages long before modern times. For some, such as the Kavalan group of "Plains Aborigines" (平埔族) from Ilan's Lanyang Plain and the northeast coast , now largely assimilated into the Han-Chinese population, it was women who led the way in choosing their partners on reaching maturity. This may reflect women's more important role and economic power in Aboriginal societies, many of which were also matrilineal.

In modern Taiwan, marriage has changed almost beyond recognition. Love-marriages are the rule and matchmakers have almost disappeared. Monogamy has been the only legal option since 1928, and homosexual lifestyles are becoming more openly practiced and accepted. Through Western influence, St. Valentine's Day is becoming more popular; nevertheless, China's traditional Lovers' Day (情人節) is still widely celebrated. Falling on the seventh day of the seventh lunar month, it commemorates the legendary story of love between the Celestial Cowherd and the Weaving Maid.

Statues of the Celestial Cowherd and Weaving Maid on the roof of Taipei's "Love Temple."

Chinese "Valentine's"

Qi Xi (七夕; Evening of the Seventh Day) is commonly known as Lovers' Day.

According to a Han dynasty legend, a young cowherd fell in love with a fairy from heaven, who was disguised as a weaving maid. They married and had two children. When her father, the Emperor of Heaven (天帝), discovered their tryst, he banished them to opposite sides of heaven, separated by the Milky Way (天河; Heaven's River).

To see the Celestial Cowherd (牛郎星) today, look for Altair, the brightest star in the constellation Aquila; for the Weaving Maid (織女星), find Vega in the constellation Lyra.

Once each year, with the Emperor's permission, they may meet, crossing a bridge constructed by sympathetic magpies (a symbol of joy). It is said that, on this day, the skies are often obscured by clouds or rain to hide the couple's shame.

This story also reflects the traditional roles of men plowing and women weaving, and symbolizes the eternal hopes of all frustrated lovers that one day they may finally be together. The idiom "cowherd and weaving maid" (牛郎織女) describes the sadness of all separated lovers.

One custom practiced on this date is for romantically-inclined young girls to break a cake of make-up into two, throwing one half onto the roof for the celestial Weaving Maid and keeping the other for their own use. Another tradition is to try and thread a needle by moonlight.

The Idea of Marriage

According to another Chinese legend, the institution of marriage originated with China's legendary ruler Fu Xi (伏羲; trad. 2852--2737 BC). He is said to have married his sister, Nü Wa(女媧) , thereby giving rise to the human race.

Traditional marriage customs and regulations are said to date back to the Duke of Zhou (周公), who lived in the 11th century BC, later assembled into the *Book of Rites* (禮記). These include six steps to be followed when getting married:

1. Proposal of Marriage.
2. Checking of Names.
3. Divining the Marriage's Destiny.
4. Arranging the Betrothal Gifts.
5. Setting of Dates.
6. Receiving the Bride.

Confucius says...

"Marry one who has not betrayed her own kin, and you may safely present her to your ancestors."* (I:13)

"Gong Ye Chang is fit to be wived. Although he was imprisoned, he was not guilty." Confucius married his own daughter to him. (V:01)

Of Nan Rong, "In a country with the Way, he would not be discarded; in a country without the Way, he would avoid capital punishment." Confucius married his brother's daughter to him. (V:02)

---

*   *The Analects of Confucius* (trans. A. Waley, 1938)

Although these are primarily social, cultural and legal codes, they are further colored with religious, mythological and superstitious characteristics.

1. Proposal of Marriage (納采)

This was mainly the work of the professional matchmaker who, knowledgeable about the status and qualities of all eligible individuals in the region, took charge of "negotiation of marriage" (議婚) and even the "proposal of marriage" (說親).

Today in Taiwan, it is illegal to make money as a marriage matchmaker, although, to judge from the open advertisements for Vietnamese and other foreign brides (who now account for around 9% of all Taiwanese brides*), and fees of up to NT$300,000, there are ways around this law.

2. Checking of Names (問名)

Until recent times, it was illegal for people of the same surname to marry. An exception could be made for people coming from far-separated regions of the empire, but even this required an imperial decree. Same-surname marriage is still sometimes frowned upon.

Even more important is the checking of a prospective bride's and groom's Eight Terms to ensure there are no cosmic impediments to the union. One prerequisite is that the total figure produced by adding all sixteen characters is even (*yin*), as odd (*yang*) numbers are inauspicious for marriage.

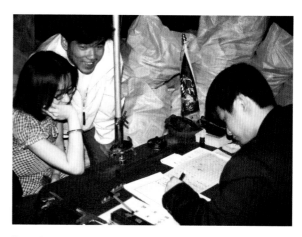

Young lovers get their Eight Terms checked for compatibility by a temple fortune-teller.

Infant girls were sometimes issued with fake birth certificates by fortune-tellers, who chose auspicious times of birth to ensure good omens for marriage (nowadays, people may time their caesarian delivery in a similar way).

The results of this comparison of Eight Terms were written on red paper and placed in front of the ancestral tablets in the home or clan shrine. Here they were worshiped for three days and, if no inauspicious events occurred, the engagement was allowed to go ahead.

In modern Taipei, prognostication of a person's chances in love and marriage is still one of the most popular reasons for visiting a temple fortune-teller.

---

* *Taipei Times* (Oct. 22, 2002)

3. Divining the Marriage's Destiny (納吉)

Further divination was carried out at a temple, traditionally by means of a wild goose (雁); nowadays by consultation with a favored deity.

Assuming that auspicious (吉) omens are divined for the marriage, when this result was reported back to the bride's family, they announced the preliminary engagement (小定). This was cemented by presentation of "small betrothal gifts" (小聘) agreed by both families through the matchmaker. Even though today's marriages are based on love, the two families will still conduct negotiations, more often inviting a relative or friend to act as informal go-between.

At this stage, only a few gifts were given to the bride-to-be, including a cash down-payment; gold-colored flowers bearing the auspicious words *sheng* (生) and *geng* (庚), lengths of red and black silk; jewelry, pork, lamb and cake; candles, incense and firecrackers; pomegranates or taro blossoms (because they contain many seeds or bloom in great numbers symbolizing a marriage blessed with many children); and two bronze rings tied together with red string to symbolize the eternal bonding of two hearts ("bronze" 銅 and "together" 同 are both pronounced *tong*). Many of these gifts are still used today in a conscious nod to tradition.

After these gifts have been handed over, the future daughter-in-law appears and serves sweet tea to her fiance's relatives (in a break from tradition, he may now accompany them). The visitors make a show of examining her rings to take an opportunity to examine her palms for broken lines which, in the past, would be sufficient cause to cancel the wedding since such lines foretold of the husband's death.

4. Arranging the Betrothal Gifts (納弊)

On an auspicious date after some time had elapsed, the rest of the betrothal gifts were presented completing the engagement (大定).

Headed by a group of musicians, the outstanding betrothal money (聘金) and innumerable ostentatious gifts were carried through the streets (行聘) to the bride's family's house. Many of these objects were of symbolic value, such as a pair of ducks, because ducks mate for life; long noodles representing a long life together; dried oranges (橘; *ju*) which pun with "auspicious" (吉; *ji*) and so forth. The money amount should not include the number four (四; *si*), which sounds like "death" (死; *si*)

A proportion of the engagement gifts and cash were returned to the groom's family on this day (the amount was agreed in advance through the matchmaker) to avoid the feeling that the bride had been bought. Even today, when money is given to the bride's family it is often returned to the groom's family or given to the newlyweds, but this cannot be taken for granted.

Nowadays a woman must be at least fifteen to become engaged; a man seventeen. Traditionally, however, a child of any age could be betrothed before birth in a practice known as "pointing at the stomach for marriage" (指腹為婚).

A bridal palanquin and sieve decorated with Eight Trigrams on display in a Taipei antiques store.

5. Setting of Dates (請期)

An auspicious date for the wedding was chosen in consultation with priests and fortune-tellers. Prayers were made to the gods, in particular to the Lord of Heaven (天公), creator of the universe, to inform him of the couple's intention to marry.

On an inauspicious day before the marriage, a little boy was chosen to bounce on the bridal bed in a ceremony known as "settling the bed" (安床), which was supposed to bring about the quick birth of a son and heir.

On her wedding day, the bride ate a last meal with her brothers and sisters, then made her final prayers to the clan ancestors, said goodbye and "left her family forever."

6. Receiving the Bride (親迎)

The times at which the bride left her childhood home and arrived at her new home were chosen with great care so that her movements accorded with cosmic harmony. Members of the groom's family turned up to collect the bride and her father threw a bucket of water behind her symbolizing that "a daughter married off is like water tossed away" (嫁出去的女兒，潑出去的水).

In one tradition which is still very much alive, a piece of pork tied to a length of bamboo or sugarcane may still be seen attached to the bride's car and, as she gets in and out, her head is covered by a ceremonial sieve decorated with Eight Trigrams and "grand ultimate" (太極) designs.

A Mercedes-Benz is often today's bride's palanquin.

The nodes of bamboo or similar decorations represent the stages of life, such as in today's wedding ceremony.

Covering the Bride with a Sieve

Once upon a time, a mother became increasingly anxious when her son failed to come home. Her local fortune-teller, Zhou Gong (周公), said that her son would die in an accident.

On her way home, her sobs were overheard by a poor young woman, "Peach Blossom Girl" (桃花女), who said she should hang pork on a length of bamboo at her door, while calling her son's name. If it rained, she should shout louder.

Finally, one rainy day, her son returned. He had been hiding in a cave when, hearing his name, he ran outside. Almost immediately, the cave collapsed.

As the Peach Blossom Girl's fame spread, Zhou Gong lost all his clients. Angry, he asked for her hand in marriage, planning to invoke evil spirits to kill her on their wedding day.

The young woman could not defy her parents' wishes even though she knew of Zhou's plans. On her wedding day, she tied a piece of pork to a length of bamboo and tied it to the back of her palanquin, and covered her head with a rice sieve on which she had drawn the Eight Trigrams credited with magical powers, customs practiced to this day, even though a bride's "palanquin" is usually a Mercedes-Benz.

Nowadays an umbrella may also be used instead of a sieve.

The bride should also carry a fan with money attached, which she throws as she enters the car. Whoever picks it up is guaranteed good fortune.

Child relatives of the groom prepare two sweet oranges, which the bride strokes to ensure her married life will be sweet and auspicious. She gives red envelopes of cash to these children and, still covered by the sieve, approaches her new home. She must step over an incense burner placed in her path, which is also said to promote the birth of many sons and grandsons, and must avoid touching the raised threshold (rarely found in modern houses), which is said to be a place where ghosts congregate.

A New Member of the Family

Her first act inside her new home is to make prayers and offerings to her husband's ancestral tablets, at which time she becomes a member of his family.

After the wedding banquet (喜宴), close friends or family of the groom often invade the marriage chamber to play pranks in a practice known as "causing trouble in the nuptial chamber" (鬧洞房) or "drinking the bride's tea" (喝新娘茶), which is said to have originated in the belief that mischievous fox spirits would cause trouble and needed to be tricked into thinking this had already been done.

Nowadays, these six steps to marriage established three millennia ago may be held on two, or even one, day, allowing everything to occur in a few hours rather than over months or, preferably, years.

Wife after Death

In one custom, if a girl dies unmarried and then appears to her parents in a dream expressing her sadness, they may procure a marriage for her. One method is to put a red envelope of money on the side of a road which, if picked up by a man, indicates that he was destined to marry her.

If the girl was already engaged at the time of death, the groom should go through with the wedding, as one Nantou high school student did after his girlfriend died in the 9-21 earthquake of 1999.

If both betrothed parties die, a marriage ceremony may be held for their spirit tablets.

Part III: Death, Mourning, Exhumation and the Afterlife

One of the strangest sights in Taipei is that of ambulances speeding dying people away from hospitals. This is because, especially for clan elders, dying at home in front of the ancestral tablet is a great honor. Moreover, it is also believed that the spirit of someone who dies far from home may suffer for eternity as a wandering ghost. Even those who die in hospital will be presented to the tablets before burial. Four exceptions are made, however. These include:

Dressed in sackcloth or white clothing, a line of relatives and friends follows the coffin to its interment.

1. A person whose father or grandfather is still alive, unless he has greatly enhanced the family prestige.

2. Children under twelve.

3. Suicides.

4. Those who die by drowning.

Death by drowning is especially disliked since it is believed that water spirits take corpses in order to effect their own reincarnation.

Cheaper than Qin Shi-huang's terracotta warriors, today's dead can still be provided with horses and soldiers by burning printed paper drawings.

Spirit World

Traditional Chinese ideas regarding the afterlife originate in the belief that human beings have a soul, which lives inside the body in the *yang* (陽) realm while a person is alive and goes to a *yin* (陰) realm after the person dies. Even in this netherworld the soul needs food, clothing, housing, transportation and the other necessities of daily life. Ideally, these are provided on a regular basis by the surviving descendents of the deceased.

Prehistoric graves in China contain the remains of household utensils, clothing, pets, and even the wives and servants that were buried together with the corpses of important individuals. By the end of the Zhou dynasty, these had been replaced by wooden and pottery replicas (俑). Today, even the ancestors of the poorest people can be looked after with replica objects made of paper, or simply sheets of paper printed with pictures of daily utensils.

Most common, however, is the burning of spirit money (神紙). Sometimes printed with dollars payable at the "Bank of Hell" (冥通銀行), this cash can be used for buying necessities or bribing the officials in hell. Also called "joss money" (pidgin English, from the Portuguese *deos,* meaning god), ghost money is burnt for ancestral spirits and deities.

Heir and Sponsor

It is correct worship by a legal heir which defines an ancestor. In return for "being mindful of one's origins and conducting due ceremonies to honor one's parents and ancestors," ancestral spirits ensure that their descendents have good fortune and protection in the human realm. Sufficient offerings also ensure that the deceased do not return to haunt the living. One of these "due ceremonies" is the burning of

Joss money may be more intricately decorated than regular cash.

incense in a censer or lighting a candle before the ancestral tablet (祖牌) on the home altar or at the clan shrine.

Confucius says...

Confucianism incorporated and expanded on these ancient concepts, using ancestor worship to uphold hierarchy and the authority of elders, maintain social control, and foster traditional attitudes.

"When alive, serve them [one's parents] according to ritual; when they die, bury them according to ritual and make sacrifices to them according to ritual." (II:05)

"When a man's father is alive, one observes his intentions; when his father dies, one observes his behavior. If for three years he does not make changes in his father's way, then he may be called filial." (I:11) and (IV:20)

Traditional coffins have an inner and outer section.

Services for the Deceased

Generally, Taipei funeral services follow Daoist conventions and are officiated by Daoist priests (道士), although Buddhist services are also practiced and Tibetan Buddhist funerals are gaining in popularity. Because of the various schools of Daoism and because the ancestors of today's Taiwanese came from many regions of mainland China, there are myriad variations to the following procedures.

The first act after a person dies is usually the symbolic breaking of a bowl, which represents the idea that the person will not eat with the family again.

Traditionally, the corpse is then laid out flat with a stone for a pillow. Nowadays, stacks of spirit money are often used, or even packs of tissue paper.

A "Heavenly Lord Censer" (天公爐) is placed beside the body, and the ancestral tablet and statues of the deities on the family altar are covered with a cloth until the body is placed in the coffin. The corpse is also covered with a white cloth, and a bowl of rice containing a duck egg is placed at the feet, into which is inserted vertically a pair of chopsticks to look like incense sticks (which explains why chopsticks must never be inserted in this manner into food on any other occasion).

A white cloth is hung outside the door (red if the deceased has reached the age of seventy, as this is considered less tragic, just as it is not necessary to cry for someone of this age or someone who has produced great-grandsons).

The corpse is watched continually day and night until the funeral to prevent cats and dogs from running beneath or jumping over, in which case it would come back to life as a zombie (殭屍).

If the person died of lung disease then the mouth is blocked with a goose egg to avoid spreading disease; if of leprosy, surrounding neighbors should not cook but instead go out to beg for food.

Cash drawable at the Bank of Hell can be used to buy essentials and bribe hell's officials.

Bribing the Judges of Hell

Ghost money should be burnt soon after death, as it will be needed quickly. This is why friends and relatives may be seen burning money at the roadside or riverbank immediately after a traffic accident or drowning. Ghost money is needed to bribe the officials of hell. Hell is seen as composed of a series of courts staffed by judges and guards who are as corruptible as their human counterparts. People judged to be good eventually pass through the courts and become ancestral spirits (or, according to Buddhist thinking, are reborn in one of the six realms of existence), while bad people stay in hell and become tormented ghosts.

The priest guides the spirit throughout the above process, singing and drawing a bridge on the floor to lead the deceased to the afterlife. A white-cloth flag bearing the name of the deceased, tied to a length of bamboo, is used to guide the dead.

At Buddhist funerals, monks and nuns recite sutras into the corpse's ear to comfort the soul in the frightening moments after death and lead it through the yin realm before rebirth.

Traditionally, there were five grades of mourning (五服) depending on level of kinship:

1. Three years for parents or husbands.
2. Twelve months for grandparents.
3. Nine months for brothers.
4. Five months for uncles and aunts.
5. Three months for more distant relatives.

Gold (金) joss money (right) is burnt for deities and ancestors; silver (銀; left) for the wandering and hungry ghosts not provided for by their own descendents.

A person does not need to be dead to buy his or her funeral attire (壽衣; longevity clothing).

Funeral

The funeral is held on a day determined auspicious in traditional farmers' "yellow" almanacs or by a *feng-shui* expert. This is usually quite soon after death, though the coffin may lie at home for months or even years. Rich people tend to be buried later; poor more quickly. Funerals for Hakkas (客家人), however, tend to be carried out soon after death.

Long-life Clothing

After death, or even just before, the corpse is dressed in five or seven garments known as "long-life clothing" (壽衣). These are sometimes given as gifts at adulthood, marriage or, more commonly, on a person's sixty-first birthday.

"Long-life clothing" tend to be traditional Han-Chinese styles, a practice said to date from the 17th century, when a Chinese official named Wu San-gui (吳三桂), like many who saw the Ming dynasty as hopelessly weak and corrupt, helped the Manchurian army invade Beijing and establish the Qing dynasty in 1644. Knowing that he would never again wear his official Ming court clothing, he asked permission to be buried in them.

Before the corpse is placed in the coffin, the latter is lined with straw and ashes to absorb fluids or humidity. Ghost paper is then added, as well as a stone or boiled egg (since it is said that a body becomes a ghost when the stone rots or the egg becomes a chicken). A piece of gold or a gem is placed in the coffin to encourage descendents to come back and exhume the body.

When the body is finally put into the coffin and covered, it is ready for taking to the communal burial plot, known as *chut swa* (出山; going to the mountain) in Taiwanese. It is carried firstly into the house's yard where, led by the priest among much praying and burning of ghost money, it is nailed shut. The priest leads the family around the coffin three times and ties it with ropes for carrying. Finally, led by the priest, a *huan-a* flag and a picture of the deceased, the procession of family and friends wearing white clothing or sackcloth moves off. Ghost money is thrown along the route and burnt at crossroads and bridges, places where ghosts are liable to be waiting.

Before burial, offerings are offered to Lord of the Land (土地公) to inform him of the death, and request his protection of the grave. Holes are made in the coffin to accelerate decomposition.

Exhumation

Six years after the burial, descendents return, exhume the body and clean the bones. These are then placed in a ceramic pot. This is then transferred to the family grave, and placed in the correct position in relation to the first ancestor, who occupies the central place of honor.

The location of graves is also of great importance, requiring an ideal confluence of wind (風; *feng*) and water (水; *shui*) to benefit both the deceased and their descendents. Ideally, this means nestling the burial urn in the curve of rolling hills and near running water. (This is origin of the practice of *feng-shui*.)

Cremation and Body-part Bags

Because of problems of land scarcity as well as the heavy financial costs of burial, cremation is becoming more widely accepted, despite its contravention of traditional views that a complete body is needed upon arrival in the next world.

It is this outlook that encouraged court eunuchs in imperial China to carry their severed genitalia in small pouches on their person.

With positive *feng-shui* at a premium, good graveyards get very crowded.

Looking to the Future
— Origins and Practice of Divination and Fortune-telling

The tools of her trade laid out, a fortune-teller near Longshan Temple is ready for the evening's clients.

For many of today's Taiwanese, hopeful or worried about what life has in store for them, divination (占卜) and fortune-telling (算命) play important roles in their lives, just as they did for their Chinese or Austronesian ancestors.

As divination in Taipei is essentially a religious practice calling on the help of deities or spirits, the best place to find a fortune-teller is near, or even inside, a temple.

From archaeological and written records, it seems that divination was originally used by the ruling class. Over the following millennia, prognostication practices disseminated gradually to other sections of society, a situation reflected in the broad spectrum of temple-goers practicing some form of divination today. Just about every technique imaginable (and unimaginable) has been and is used for discerning the future.

The following pages outline some of the more important and more interesting examples.

1. Oracle Bone Divination

One of the earliest techniques was probably scapulimancy, that is, the drilling of holes in the shoulder blades of ox and deer and, later, in turtle shells, into which red-hot brands were inserted until the bones cracked in a characteristic 卜 shape (from which the modern character for divination is derived).

This was accompanied by rituals and preceded by asking one or a series of yes-no questions. The cracks were then analyzed and the answer interpreted. By at least the 3rd millennium BC, specialists

Selecting a numbered divination lot.

China's oldest systematic writing is found on bones used for divination in the Shang dynasty. (This example is in the Institute of History and Philology Museum.)

in reading these stress fractures already constituted a distinct occupational group. (The choice of deer, sheep, pig or cattle bones perhaps depended on the totem animals of different Neolithic tribes.) For the Chinese, the turtle is a symbol of longevity and wisdom; its curved upper shell is also likened to the "circular heavens," its underside to the "flat earth."

The questions asked, the diviners' interpretations and sometimes the outcomes were recorded on the bones and shells. Known as Oracle Bone Script, these are the oldest systematic form of Chinese writing discovered to date and provide the richest source of information about Chinese society in the 2nd millennium BC.

Important Questions

Questions asked by the Shang kings include:

1. Matters concerning the royal household such as when would be the best date for the queen to become pregnant.
   One example concerns the royal concubine, Fu Hao (婦好):
   prognostication: if she gave birth on a *ding* (丁) day, it would be very good.
   Result: she gave birth on the *jia-yin* (甲寅) day, it was not good, she gave birth to a girl.*)
2. Matters of national importance such as whether to go to war against a neighboring state and
   which general should take command.
3. Agricultural concerns such as whether it would rain the next day.
4. The interpretation of royal dreams.

All matters relating to the king were, by definition, religious questions since the Shang rulers were theocrats whose legitimacy rested on their ability to communicate with god (上帝) through the spirits of their ancestors, the earlier Shang kings. Many inquiries therefore concerned the appropriate sacrifices that should be made to ancestors. Moreover, since illness or misfortune in the human realm

Oracle bones also show the holes drilled and resultant 卜-shaped cracks.

---

* Hsu Ya-hwei, *Ancient Chinese Writing,* National Palace Museum 2002, p29.

was thought to be caused by disgruntled ancestral spirits, divination was used to find the correct offerings and prayers needed to appease them.

2. Clutching at Straws

Being cheaper than turtle plastrons, many of which were imported from southern neighbors, milfoil stalks allowed other social classes to engage in divination.

It is unclear how milfoil stalks (*Achillea sibirica,* but probably from an early date also bamboo slips) were used in antiquity. The earliest description comes from late Zhou dynasty sources, which mention 49 stalks divided randomly into two groups. From these, groups of four stalks were removed repeatedly until four or less remained, which thus generated either a solid *yang* line (_____) for odd numbers or broken *yin* line (__ __) for even numbers. Repetition of this process produced hexagrams of six such lines.

Fu Xi inventing the Eight Trigrams as shown on an ROC postage stamp.

Milfoil Divination and the *Yi-Jing*

According to legend, trigrams were discovered by Fu-Xi, and divinatory interpretations put forward by Duke Wen (文公) at the beginning of the Zhou dynasty. These were developed into the *Book of Changes* (易經; *Yi-Jing*), which lists all sixty-four hexagram possibilities arising by combining six solid or broken lines. It is still the most common text used with milfoil-style divination.

The Yi-Jing, described by one scholar as, "an assorted and jumbled compilation of omens, rhymed proverbs, riddles and paradoxes, snatches of song and story, drawn from popular lore and archaic traditions of divination,"* provides each hexagram with a name, activity, state, situation, quality, emotion or relationship, as well as a "judgment" and a "reading."

The hexagrams are said to represent changes inherent in the universe (易 "*yi*" means "change"); their interpretation therefore offers understanding into these changes, future as well as past.

Drawing Lots

Not only is the *Yi-Jing* still popular, but a modern version of milfoil selection is found in most temples throughout the city, indeed, throughout the Chinese world. Using a large drum filled with bamboo sticks known as the "lots barrel" (籤桶) (smaller, hand-held versions are common among

---

* Richard J. Smith, Fortune-Tellers and Philosophers - Divination in Traditional Chinese Society, p.19, SMC Publishing.

fortune-tellers' paraphernalia), the "drawing of lots" (抽籤) to discern the will of heaven may be officiated by a Daoist priest (道士) or, more commonly, is part of a DIY method performed by temple visitors themselves.

Having made reverent prayers and offerings to the spirit or ancestor of choice, and concentrating hard on the question to be asked, the petitioner mixes the bamboo sticks with his or her fingers until moved to choose one at random. This stick is inscribed with a number, which corresponds to a piece of paper found in a numbered drawer of a nearby cabinet, or hung on a board.

The number of sticks varies from temple to temple. If there are 64 sticks, a temple is probably using

A father teaches his child to select an omen lot at a Taipei temple.

Checking the reading from the numbered drawers may require assistance from a temple consultant.

the *Yi-Jing* readings. The 100 readings used at Xing Tian Gong (行天宫; also "Hsing Tien Temple") date back some eight hundred years.

> Although roman numerals (a) might be used, more likely are Chinese numbers (b) or the more complex forms (c).
>
> a) 1 2 3 4 5 6 7 8 9 10 100
> b) 一 二 三 四 五 六 七 八 九 十 百
> c) 壹 貳 參 肆 伍 陸 柒 捌 玖 拾 佰

Written in archaic script or with obscure references or poetry, the prognostications can even be difficult for Chinese people to understand. Sometimes a vernacular translation (白話) is provided on the reverse and many larger temples will have specialist staff on hand to help with interpretation.

In this temple the readings are hung in order on a board.

3. Divinatory Blocks
— Democratic, Accessible and Immediate

Nowadays, divination is open to all and the simplest methods do not even require subsequent interpretation of enigmatic antique Chinese quotations. Perhaps the most accessible is "throwing blocks" (擲筊; *zhi jiao*), better known locally by the Taiwanese "*bwa-bwey.*"

Rather like tossing a coin, bwa-bwey involves asking a yes-no question. Instead of coins, two crescent-moon blocks of bamboo or wood are used. Curved on one side and flat on the other, they are usually painted red.

A block that lands flat side up represents *yang;* curved side up represents *yin.* Both blocks land-

Buckets of divination blocks are found on temple altars.

ing curved side upwards is the negative-answer "*yin* blocks" (陰筊); two flat sides facing upwards is "laughing blocks" (笑筊) and means that the question should be rephrased; while one flat and one curved side showing is "sagely blocks" (聖筊) and represents a clear "yes."

If the blocks have an equal 50% chance of landing either *yin* or *yang,* then throwing the two blocks should give a 1:1:2 ratio of "no": "maybe": "yes." Some people, wishing to reduce this advantage, ask the same

Results of throwing blocks might be "sagely blocks" (left), "*yin* blocks" (center) or "laughing blocks" (right).

Holding the blocks gently and facing the god she wishes to ask, the petitioner concentrates on a single question.

Origins of the *Jiao* (筊)

Among various origins suggested, one is that they represent the *yin* and *yang* halves of the Grand Ultimate (太極) symbol of Daoism.

Another story, deriving from the Yuan dynasty book *Twenty-four Filial Exemplars* (二十四孝), tells of an unfilial son who, having caused his mother's drowning and failed to find her body, in repentance cut a floating plank into two halves to divine his mother's will.

Yet another suggests that *jiao* derived from ancient people's use of oyster shells as money. Shells may have been used as divine offerings, and then for divination. Because shells are fragile they were replaced by blocks of bamboo.

The word 筊 also sounds similar to 教 (*jiao;* to teach), and perhaps also derived from the idea that they provide people with the "teachings" of the spirits and gods.

question two or three times; others say that once is enough because the deity might lose patience if his or her response is questioned.

Questions asked range from life-transforming subjects such as whom to marry or whether to move out of one's parents' house, to simple ones such as whether an ancestor has eaten enough of the offerings, in which case they may be taken home for consumption by the living.

Sometimes casting blocks is a group activity, presided over by a temple elder or Daoist priest. On such occasions, one person reads out the questions, one throws the blocks, one records the results, etc., as an excited audience looks on.

4. Scented Messages from the Gods

Other temple-based divination techniques are known as "Forecasting bad and good fortune by burning incense" (燒香預測禍福).

One such method is based on the relative speeds at which three simultaneously-lit sticks of incense burn.

For example:

If the right stick burns much faster than the other two:

Someone will die within one month or someone will be injured within six months.

If the right stick burns only marginally faster than the other two:

A family member will "wear mourning clothes" within seven days.

If the left stick burns fastest, the right next so and the central stick slowest:
Financial gain within ten days.
If the central stick burns very fast and the outer two hardly at all:
Within seven days a bad person will arrive and dispute "right or wrong" with you.
If the central stick burns slightly faster than the outer two:
Someone will arrive within three days bringing some good news.

Details are published in temple handbooks, including those of the Guandu Temple (關渡宮) or the Ji-yi Temple (集義宮) in Wanhua.

5. Twitching Eyes

Sufficient empirical observation of any phenomena combined with meticulous record taking allowed the Chinese to devise innumerable systems of prognostication. One unusual method is "Divination Method using Twitches of the Eyelid" (眼皮跳動占卜法).

No theoretical explanation is offered as to why gods or spirits might go about twitching a person's eyelid; nevertheless, divinatory readings are offered for involuntary twitches of the left and right eye at different times of the day.

Examples include:
Twitch of the left eye (7-9 a.m.):
An important guest will pay a visit.
Twitch of the right eye (7-9 a.m.):
Very possible that something will be lost by accident.
Twitch of the right eye (9-11 a.m.):
You will hear some sad news.
Twitch of the left eye (1-3 p.m.):
You will get some money at an unexpected time.
Twitch of the right eye (9-11 p.m.):
You should pay careful attention to the wording of letters of litigation.

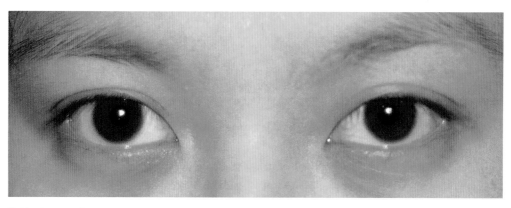

Waiting for a twitch.

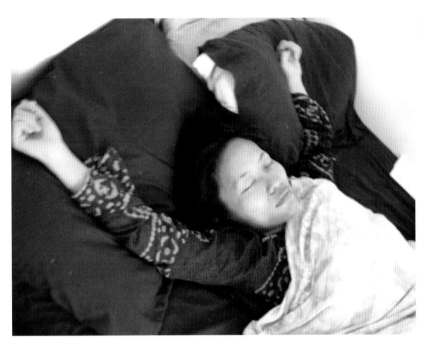

Dreaming
(of victory perhaps).

Similar methods include divination on the basis of heartbeat (心跳占卜法), sneezing (打噴嚏占卜法), buzzing in the ears (耳鳴占卜法) and, more recently, blood type (血型占卜法).

6. Dreaming and Time Travel

During the Shang dynasty, interpretation was made of kings' dreams; in later times, this was extended to all classes (though possibly, in ancient times no one else thought to record their dreams). Moreover, just as the kings' dreams were seen as messages from the spirits of deceased ancestors ((legend maintains that King Shun (舜 c 2200 BC) decided to abdicate his throne after analysis of his dreams)), dream interpretation (夢占) today is still based on a similar assumption.

Life will be Like a Dream

Chinese analysis of dreams is very different from Freudian and other Western practices. Rather than looking for psychological explanations of a person's character or behavior, they were considered to be omens of the future.

That dreams might predict the future is based on the belief that, during sleep, the *hun* (魂), higher, spiritual part of the soul, may leave the body through a hole in the top of the head and wander the earth, sometimes unseen and sometimes in animal form.

The natural world, with future changes inherent in it, invokes certain responses in the dreaming soul. More importantly, while wandering, the soul may encounter ghosts and spirits, or the *hun* of other people, all of which may impart information about otherwise unknowable events.

There are numerous handbooks of dream interpretations, the following examples come from a list of more than one thousand dream subjects and prognostications given in one called the *Mastery of a Myriad Techniques* (萬法精通).

1. A cloudless dawn

Has very auspicious portents

2. Clouds parting and the sun shining through

Suggests the dispersal of bad affairs

3. Frost or snow falling

Important matters will not come to fruition

4. A wife with disheveled hair

Means she is having an affair

5. A new door

Heralds the birth of a great child

6. Lighting a fire in the hearth

Means the dreamer will become famous

7. Riding in a boat and seeing the sun or moon

Implies one will gain official position or employment

8. Being naked

Suggests things will go smoothly

9. Wearing new clothes

Announces promotion to new position

10. Eating garlic

Means that calamity or injury is imminent

Historical Dreams

History books are full of tales in which dreams figure prominently.

1. Cao Cao (曹操), ruler of the 3rd century CE Wei (魏) dynasty, dreamt of three horses (馬) feeding from a single trough (槽; cao). He interpreted this as meaning that three members of the Sima (司馬) family threatened to devour the Cao empire. He curtailed their power and even warned his son to keep an eye on them.

2. Li Yuan (李淵), first emperor of the Tang dynasty, dreamt that he fell under his bed and was eaten by maggots. Initially discouraged in his plans to overthrow the Sui dynasty, "falling under the bed" was subsequently interpreted by a subordinate as meaning "beneath the steps" (a term used in addressing the Emperor) and "being eaten by maggots" as "the masses depending on him for their food." He then raised an army and ... the rest is history.

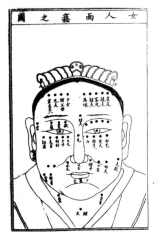
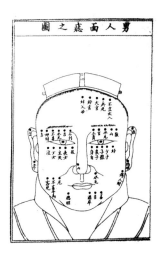

The position of marks on the face is believed to correlate to one's fate (inauspiciously located birthmarks are often removed).

7. Auspicious Names

Even though names are chosen by parents or family elders, and surnames are generally passed down from the father and certainly cannot be chosen, it is nevertheless believed that some names are more auspicious than others. Since names are thought to reveal one's destiny and also influence it, changing one's personal name is widespread.

Interpretation of one's existing name or suggestions for a new one generally come from fortune-tellers or books specializing in that subject. The following notes come from the *Collected Canon of Surnames and Names* (姓名彙典).

Innate and Acquired

For divinatory purposes, the surname is considered "innate" (先天) while the given names are "acquired" (後天). Those entrusted with selecting a baby's name must take great care to find an auspicious (吉) name, therefore, except when a baby almost dies at birth or if its parents are very old, in which case, a bad (凶) name will be intentionally chosen to make malevolent spirits think the infant is unworthy of their attention. Although rare today, there are not a few elderly people bearing names such names as "Mountain Boar" (山豬) "Dog's Droppings" (狗屎) or "Beggar" (乞食). Similarly, boys are sometimes given girls' names.

The essence of choosing auspicious names lies in a balance of *yin* and *yang*, harmony of the Five Elements and calculations of the numbers of strokes used in writing the character.

The surname Lin (林), for example, has eight strokes; Ma(馬) has 10; Chen (陳) has eleven and Zheng (鄭) has fifteen. Even numbers are *yin*, odd numbers are *yang*, so Chinese characters with even or odd numbers of strokes are ascribed a fundamental nature accordingly. A typical three-character Chinese name should have ideally a mix of *yin* and *yang* names rather than all of one. The name of the ROC's first president, Chiang Kai-shek (蔣介石), is well-balanced, with one *yin* character (介-4

Family names—this one is Su (蘇)— cannot be changed, and affect the course of one's life.

strokes) surrounded by two *yang* characters (蔣-15 strokes and 石-5 strokes), as is his style name 蔣中正 (Jiang Zhong-zheng).

Every character, in addition to being either *yin* or *yang,* is also assigned to one of the Five Elements: metal, wood, water, fire or earth. This does not seem to be as simple as might be imagined. According to the *Collected Canon of Surnames and Names,* "metal" (金) belongs to the wood element (木) rather than metal; "fire" (火) belongs to the water element (水) as does the "wood" element (木); "earth" (土) belongs to fire (火); and "water" (水) belongs to metal (金) and so forth.

To make matters more complicated, the "significant" under which each character is classified is also believed to exert an influence, so that as well as belonging to the water element, "wood" also has wood influences, as does the surname Lin which is otherwise ascribed to the fire element, or Yang (楊), which belongs to the earth element.

Each of the Five Elements is in harmony with some Elements and in disharmony with others, and each character in a person's name should be chosen to harmonize with the surname (which cannot be changed) and with each other.

Furthermore, the total number of strokes in the name is said to represent a person's "general character" (總格), while those of the surname and second character represent the "human" personality (人格); surname alone is the "heavenly" inherent personality (天格); the second and third characters represent the "earthly" personality (地格); and the total of first and third are which is the "external" personality (外格).

According to the *Collected Canon of Surnames and Names,* President Chiang's name, with a total of 24 strokes, means he has a "general character" that is auspicious (吉), "blessed with both talent and wisdom, able to attain both wealth and high status, whose sons and grandsons will continue in good fortune."

Interpretation of characters (測字) and analysis of surname and name (相姓名) figure highly on this fortune-teller's hoarding.

8. Interpretation of Words

Chinese surnames are not a separate class from other characters, so it is not surprising that there are numerous other techniques of fortune-telling based on the interpretation of characters" (測字) or "dissection of characters" (拆字).

One method requires a client to choose a character at random from a selected text. This is then analyzed according to systematic and intuitive principles. These include the division of characters into yin and yang and Five Elements (as above), but also use traditional ideas and prejudices. For example, all words containing the "female" element (女) are disliked, even if having positive meaning such as "good" (好) or "wonderful"(妙), because 女 appears in too many negative words, such as "jealous" (妒), "absurd" (妄), "evil" (奸), "slave" (奴) and so forth.

This is just the beginning, however. One example of a word chosen randomly by a fortune-teller's client was 豐 (*feng*), ostensibly an auspicious word, meaning "abundant." However, character dissection resulted in 山 (*shan*) meaning "mountain," a pair of 丰 (*feng*) "good-looking," and 豆 (*dou*) "bean." This was interpreted as: hillsides are the location of graves, 丰丰 looks like trees sealing (also *feng* 封) one in, and 豆 derived originally as a pictograph of a ritual vessel for worshiping deceased ancestors, all of which led the fortune-teller to interpret the auspicious-sounding character 豐 as a premonition of death.*

Taken to extremes, the surname Zhu (朱) also meaning red, can produce 二 "two," 人 "person," 未 "not yet," 牛 "ox," 牙 "tooth," 才 "talent," 木 "wood" and 午 "noon."

The scope for personal interpretation is large, therefore.

9. The "Eight Terms"

Marco Polo says...

"As soon as a child is born the father or the mother has a record made of the day and the minute and the hour at which he was born, and under what constellation and planet, so that everyone knows his horoscope. Whenever anyone intends to make a journey into another district or a business deal, he consults the astrologer and tells him his horoscope; and the astrologer tells him whether it is good to undertake or not.

... "When a marriage is planned, the astrologers first investigate whether the bridegroom and bride are born under concordant planets. If so, it is put into effect; if not it is called off. Great numbers of these astrologers, or rather magicians, are to be found on every square of the city."[+]

---

* *Mastery of a Myriad Techniques* (萬法精通) publ. Chuan-yuan Publications (泉源出版社), p.270.
+ *The Travels of Marco Polo; trans.* R.E. Latham, p.195; Penguin 1958.

What Marco Polo recorded in the 13th century was calculation of the Eight Terms (八字). It still forms the basis of numerous fortune-telling techniques.

Pairs of characters, one each from the list of Heavenly Stems (天干) and Earthly Branches (地支) are ascribed to the time, day, month and year (but not minute) of birth. These are arranged in a table (命盤) and used to fathom other characters which are added in surrounding "mansions" (宮).

Each mansion relates to a specific aspect such as basic fate, health, occupation, family, moving home and so forth. Constellations and planets playing an important role are listed for each mansion.

Even for Non-believers

Even people who do not believe in divination will send a copy of their Eight Terms to future in-laws before getting married, although it is unlikely that a wedding will be canceled if problems were found when "matching the eight terms" (合八字) of a prospective bride and groom. In the past and possibly still today, it was not uncommon for babies to be given "fake" birth times or dates to ensure an auspicious Eight Terms.

Although not able to speak, birds (鳥) can be trained to select a person's fortune (卜).

10. Bird Divination (靈鳥卜卦)

It is quite common to see small caged birds sitting on a fortune-teller's table.

The birds, typically Java sparrow (*Oryzornia oryzivara;* 白文鳥), are trained to step forward and select a piece of paper after the petitioner has thought of a question he or she would like to ask. The fortune-teller will then discuss the prophesy.

Coincidentally, Taiwan's Aboriginal people also used a bird-related method of divination. "They reverence to the utmost degree of superstitious veneration the chirp and movements of little birds. Should any expedition be under consideration--especially hunting, and most of all head-hunting-- they will go out and throw sticks up into some tree and disturb the birds. Should the chirp be a certain

A Taipei citizen checks out the "wind and clouds" for possible rain but not for the results of any future wars as her ancestors might have done.

sound and their flight a certain direction, nothing could induce the chief to call out his braves."*

11. Interpretations of Winds and Clouds

Chinese veneration of nature and worship of natural forces also led to the belief that natural phenomena are not random but, rather, offer insight into the heavenly realm.

In ancient times, such phenomena as the shape and timing of clouds, and the timing, speed and direction of winds, were used to predict the will of heaven and, therefore, future events, especially those relating to the Chinese emperor, who was seen as the "Son of Heaven" (天子). Since the emperor's most important functions included the waging of war and feeding his people, it was expected that omens relevant to these affairs would be visible in the sky. Winds were used for prognostication about the forthcoming harvest; clouds about military affairs.

---

* G.L.MacKay, *From Far Formosa,* Oliphant, Anderson and Ferrier, Edinburgh and London, 1896
(Reprinted SMC, Taipei 1998) p.259.

Feng-shui compasses can include many rings of information.

12. *Feng-shui* and Other Geomantic Practices

This idea that *qi* (氣) energy plays a key part in cosmic processes also led to the development of geomantic techniques, best known of which is *feng-shui.*

Increasingly in vogue in the West, *feng-shui* thus started life as another branch of divination, seeking through physical phenomena, to discern the will of heaven and its implications for humankind. In particular, *feng-shui* experts sought to optimize the siting of graves (indeed, *feng-shui* is still the Hakka word for "grave").

Concerns over correct burial can be traced to early Zhou texts such as the *Book of Rites* (禮記) and became a key aspect of filial piety. As the *Classic of Filial Piety* (孝經) states, "[The filial son] determines the burial place [of his parents] by divination and puts them to rest"*.

Change

Chinese see the cosmos as characterized by change. Any disruption in cosmic forces, such as might occur when building a new grave or house, may affect the local balance of *qi,* leading to possible misfortune or illness. *Feng-shui* experts are, therefore, "doctors of the earth"+ and, indeed, often employ medical metaphors in discussing the "treatments" needed before building (or demolition) may go ahead. Local *qi,* like that of the human body, is defined as "living" (生氣), in bright, refreshing, uplifting places, or "dead" (死氣), in decaying, depressed locations.

---

* Richard J. Smith, *Fortune-Tellers and Philosophers - Divination in Traditional Chinese Society,* p.132, SMC Publishing.

+ Richard J. Smith, *Fortune-Tellers and Philosophers - Divination in Traditional Chinese Society,* p.131, SMC Publishing.

Differing Schools

By late imperial times there were two main schools of *feng-shui,* although both traced their origins to the 3rd century diviner Guo Pu (郭璞; 276-324).

One developed in Jiangxi, an area characterized by dramatic landforms, high hills and deep troughs. Here, *feng-shui* came to emphasize the position and orientation of these forms, to determine the pairings of dragons and lairs, alluvial formations and water. The other, which arose in the flatter Fujian Province, and is based on heavenly bodies, trigrams and makes great use of the diviner's compass (羅盤), which, in addition to a south-pointing needle has a series of concentric rings inscribed with symbols representing various concepts of space and time (such as *yin* and *yang,* the Five Elements, Eight Trigrams, ten Celestial Stems and twelve Earthly Branches (天干地支), twenty-eight lunar mansions (宿), sixty-four hexagrams and so forth). Today's experts in Taipei make use of the teachings of both schools as well as their own intuition.

Mirrors, here combined with Fu Xi's Eight Trigrams, are considered a powerful force in home *feng-shui.*

Sited at the end of a main thoroughfare (a big no-no in *feng-shui*), Taipei City Hall draws on the auspicious power of a Double-Ten design (celebrating the Xin-hai revolution which began on October 10th, 1911).

Magical Powers

Complimenting such "scientific" approaches are the even more mystical aspects that ascribe supernatural powers to revered objects such as the eight trigrams, swords and lions, and mirrors. Apparently, mirrors are good at bouncing *qi* around corners as well as light, though their use above doors and gateways is associated with the popular belief that evil spirits are frightened away by their own image.

Seemingly, even *qi* can be tricked. If a doorway is "too small" and cannot be enlarged to allow *qi* to flow well, it might be made to "appear larger." On the other hand, where *qi* flows too well, it may be better to slow it down. Potted plants and tanks of fish are said to do this, so their use in shop and office design may not be merely for decoration.

Many *feng-shui* handbooks talk at length about what things look like. Rooms that taper are "knife-shaped" and, therefore, dangerous to the occupant. Animal-shaped landforms or buildings are auspicious or inauspicious corresponding to the status accorded that animal in Chinese culture; better a tiger, dragon or turtle than a pig, dog or chicken, whatever a chicken-shaped house might look like.

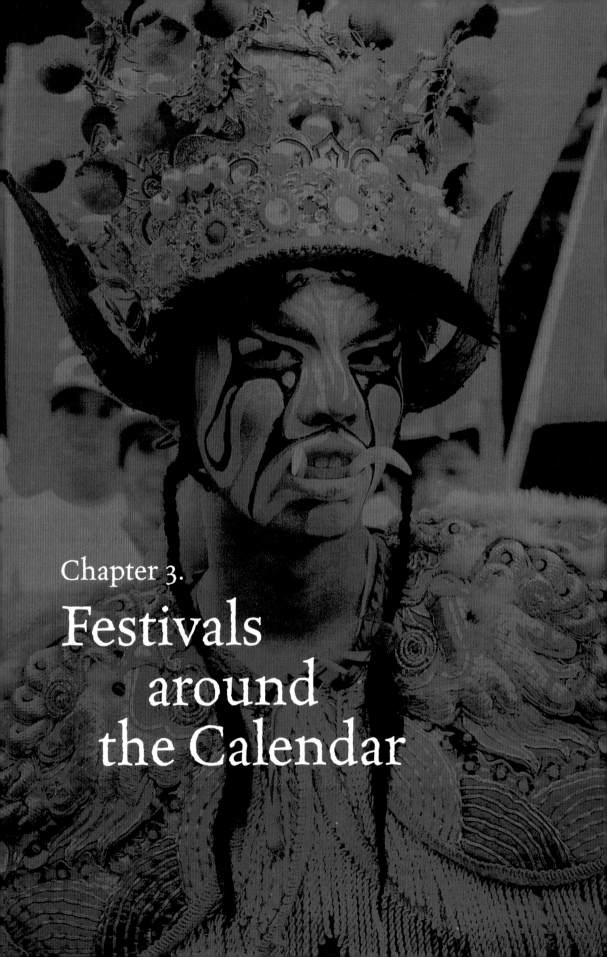

Chapter 3.
Festivals around the Calendar

Introduction to the Chinese Lunisolar Calendar

There are two main problems to overcome when drawing up a calendar: 1. reconciliation of the irreconcilable mathematics of stellar phenomena, and 2. starting the clock.

1. Horrible Fractions

A year is the time it takes for the earth to orbit the sun. This affects vegetation growth, animal behavior and, therefore, human practices such as hunting, gathering and agriculture.

A month is the time the moon takes to orbit the earth and influences tides and, probably, mood and menstruation.

A day is the time it takes for the earth to revolve on its axis, which influences our sleep patterns and has obvious uses in reckoning day-to-day activities.

There are 365 days, 5 hours, 48 minutes and about 46 seconds (c. 365.242199 days) in a solar year, and 29.53059 days in a month. Any attempt to calculate years, months and days in terms of each other, therefore, involves horrible fractions. All calendars, from Neolithic times onwards, have sought to reconcile these phenomena.

Many ancient cultures in the West concerned themselves with accurate measurements of the solar year. The Tao (Yami) Aborigines of Taiwan's Orchid Island, whose livelihood is closely tied to the flying fish, marry a calendar of lunar phases with the annual movement of that fish. Worldwide, the most widespread approach has been to combine the sun and moon's phases in a lunisolar calendar.

One Chinese discovery was that 235 lunar months every nineteen years (i.e. twelve months in a normal year and seven extra months every nineteen years) gave a reasonable approximation of 365.2467 days in the average year. The extra months are known as *run-yue* (閏月) and may occur anywhere in the year.

2. Shifting Start

One effect of the Chinese emphasis on months is that, viewed from the perspective of the sun's position (i.e. from the solar year), the 1st day of the 1st month varies by as much as a fortnight in either direction.

There is, therefore, a subsidiary solar calendar primarily for use by farmers, whose activities must follow the sun's movements. Known as the Twenty-four Solar Terms (二十四節氣), it includes periods such as the "Waking of Insects" (驚蟄; Feb.4-19), "Grain in Beard" (芒種; Jun. 6-21), "Greater Heat" (大暑; Jul. 23-Aug. 8), "Frost's Descent" (霜降; Oct. 23-Nov.7), "Winter Solstice" (冬至; Dec 21-Jan.6) and "Pure and Bright" (清明; Apr. 5-20), the first day of which is better known in Taiwan as Tomb-sweeping Festival.

Nowadays in Taipei, two New Years are celebrated, January 1st (元旦; first dawn) and Chinese New Year, about a month later.

Calendar of Some Major Religious Dates

Lunar (month/day)	Solar (month/day)	Event	Notes
正月			
1/1		Chinese New Year (農曆春節)	
1/1		Birth of Maitreya Buddha (彌勒佛)	Buddha Yet-to-Come
1/1		Birth of Celestial Venerable of the Primordial Beginning (元始天尊)	Daoist deity
1/3		Rats' Wedding Day (老鼠結婚日)	
1/4		Welcome Deities' Return (接神)	from meeting with Jade Emperor
1/6		Birth of Qingshui Zu-shi (清水祖師)	Song dynasty monk
1/9		Jade Emperor's Birthday (玉皇大帝)	chief Daoist deity
1/13		Sacrifice to Guan Di (關帝)	God of War &c.
1/15		Lantern Festival (元宵)	
1/15		Heavenly Official's Birth (上元天官)	
1/15		Sacrifice to Pan-Gu (盤古)	creator of the world
二月			
2/2		Ceremony to Tudi Gong (土地公)	Lord of the Land
2/3		Birth of Wen-Chang (文昌)	worshiped by students
三月			
3/3		Birth of Supreme Emperor of the Dark Heaven (玄天上帝)	
	April 5	Tomb-sweeping Festival (清明節)	
	Apr. 10-18	Water-sprinkling Festival (潑水節)	Buddha's birth
3/15		Birth of Baosheng Da-di (保生大帝)	
3/19		Birth of Tai-yang Xing-jun (太陽星君)	Sun Deity
3/20		Birth of Zhu-sheng Niang-niang (註生娘娘)	Madame Registrar of Births
3/23		Birthday of Ma-zu (媽祖)	Queen of Heaven
3/28		Sacrifice to Emperor of the Eastern Peak (東嶽大帝)	

Deities' statues are carried around town to celebrate each other's birthdays.

四月

| 4/8 | Cleansing Buddha Festival (浴佛節) | |
| 4/26 | Sacrifice to Shen-Nong (神農大帝) | Mythical emperor; god of agriculture and medicine |

五月

5/5	Dragon Boat Festival (端午節)	
5/13	Sacrifice to City God (城隍爺)	Xia-hai (霞海) Temple
5/18	Sacrifice at Chih-nan Temple (指南宮)	Muzha
5/18	Birth of Zhang Dao-ling (張道陵)	Patriarch of Religious Daoism

六月

| 6/19 | Guanyin attains enlightenment (觀音得道) | Mahayana bodhisattva also worshiped in popular religion |
| 6/24 | Birthday of Guan Di (關帝) | |

七月

7/1		Opening of Ghost Gates (鬼門開)	Start of Ghost Month
7/7		Lovers' Day	
7/15		Pu-du Festival (普渡)	For salvation of hungry ghosts
7/15		Earthly Official's Birth (中元地官)	
7/30		Closing of Ghost Gates (鬼門關)	End of Ghost Month

八月

8/15		Birth of Tudi Gong (土地公)	Lord of the Land
8/15		Mid-Autumn Festival (中秋節)	Also ceremonies for Old Man under the Moon (月下老人) and Moon Goddess.
	Sept. 28	Birth of Confucius (孔子)	

九月

9/9		Double Yang Festival (重陽節)	
	Oct. 25	Sacrifice to City God (城隍爺)	Taiwan Provincial City God Temple (14 Wuchang St.)

十月

10/5		Birth of Bodhidhama (菩提達摩)	
10/15		Water Official's Birth (下元水官)	
10/22		Birth of King of Qingshan (青山王).	

十一月

11/17		Offering to Amita Buddha (阿彌陀佛)	Pureland School
	Dec. 21	Winter solstice (冬至)	

臘月

12/16		*Wei-ya* (尾牙)	
12/23		Offering to Kitchen God (灶神)	
12/24		Sending off of deities (送神)	for meeting with Jade Emperor
12/30		Chinese New Year's Eve (除夕)	

Chinese New Year

The "Spring Festival" (春節) or "Crossing the Year" (過年) is the main event of the Chinese calendar.

Tooth-tail

Celebrations start a couple of weeks earlier with the *wei-ya* (尾牙; tooth-tail). *Ya* (牙; no one seems to remember the term's origin) is a twice-monthly offering to Lord of the Land (土地公), originally on the 1st and 15th (new moon and full moon) of each month but nowadays more commonly on the 2nd and 16th. Most evident today are the roadside offerings by shopkeepers and office workers of incense and foodstuffs, but traditionally "making *ya*" (做牙) also included a meal for the staff. This generosity is continued on the last ya of the year, on or around the 16th day of the 12th lunar month (which is generally known as *la-yue* 臘月). Bosses or department heads organize a banquet for their workers and customers, a practice said to date from China's imperial past when government bureaucracies closed over New Year.

Lion dancing is practiced at New Year and all major festivities and temple celebrations.

Departing Deities and Departed Ancestors

On the 24th day of the *la* month, the kitchen god and other deities return to heaven to make their annual reports to the Jade Emperor.

On New Year's Eve (除夕), the family gathers together "around the hearth" (圍爐) for the main family feast, when an additional place is set for absent relatives including deceased ancestors.

New Year's Day (初一; beginning 1st) is celebrated by Daoists as the birthday of the Celestial Venerable of the Primordial Beginning (元始天尊), and by Buddhists as the birthday of the "Buddha Yet to Come" (彌勒佛).

It is often said that firecrackers originated in the custom of scaring away the monster *nian* (年), which came out of the sea on New Year's Eve to eat people and prevent the arrival of the new year. For the same reason, Taipei's Longshan Temple has midnight drumming.

Spring couplets, which are pairs of auspicious expressions hung on either side of the front door, are also said to represent the repulsion of evil spirits. Originally they were made of peach-wood, which is accredited with magical powers.

The deities return from heaven on the 6th day of the year, and the Jade Emperor's birthday is celebrated on the 9th.

The 15th is Lantern Festival (元宵節), a major event in the calendar but not a religious one. It is also the "Upper yuan" (上元), when birthday celebrations are offered to the Heavenly Official (天官), as well as a day of offerings to Pan-Gu (盤古), creator of the universe.

Temples are busy throughout the festival period and, with stalls set up nearby selling traditional foods, make a good place to soak up the atmosphere of the original "holy-day."

Firecrackers

Large amounts of firecrackers are lit on many festive occasions to create a "hot and noisy" atmosphere, explained by scholars as an intentional stimulation of *yang* to drive out the *yin* of the netherworld.

This is particularly true of Chinese New Year's Eve when firecrackers seem to explode throughout the night. This is traced back to the mythological monster *nian* (年) said to emerge from the sea, eat people and prevent the arrival of the new year (年), who is kept at bay by the explosive sounds and also the color red.

Although gunpowder was added after its invention during the Tang dynasty as a byproduct of alchemists' search for an elixir of immortality, sections of bamboo thrown on a fire originally sufficed. This is captured in the Chinese word "exploding bamboo" (爆竹).

Auspicious spring couplets, derived from talismans hung around doors to keep evil spirits away, are still widely popular.

Ancestral Master of Qing-shui

6th day of the 1st lunar month (正月6日)

One lively religious event over the New Year period is the birthday celebrations for Qing-shui Zu-shi (清水祖師). Sacrifices of animals (including huge hogs at Sanxia's temple in Taipei County), theater performances, and temple courtyards busy with worshipers, food vendors, and *dang-ki* (divinatory boys) beating themselves with gruesome weapons all make this one of the major religious festivals of the whole year.

Monk, Butcher or "Firewood Collector"

A great variety of stories surround the "Ancestral Master of Qing-shui."

One story is that his original name was Chen Zhao-ying (陳昭應) and that he was born in Fujian Province, and that he tonsured as a monk at a young age and attained enlightenment. Later in the Ming dynasty during a great drought, people prayed to him for rain, after which his fame spread further afield.

A statue of Ancestral Master Qing-shui and incense from the main temple in Fujian arrive in Danshui (temple mural).

Another tells that he was born in the Song dynasty and, being from a poor family, that he became a temple servant. Eventually becoming a monk in Qing-shui Yan (清水巖; Pure Water Crag), he came across a rock-hole issuing forth rice, which he distributed to working people. People built a temple in his name.

A third explains why he is portrayed with a black face. Apparently, when his sister-in-law was in confinement after childbirth and could not go out to fetch firewood, he put himself onto the fire.

A fourth legend recounts how, as a butcher who slaughtered animals, Mazu (媽祖) appeared to him and told him he could never become a deity. At this, he cut out and washed his own stomach and intestines, and presented them to the goddess, who was impressed.

Taipei's Qing-shui Zu-shi Temple in Wanhua district apparently started its Taiwan existence in Danshui. A Mr. Weng (翁) had brought a statue of the Ancestral Master from Fujian to Taiwan, and worshiped it in his home. During the Sino-French War (1884), the commander-in-chief of the army petitioned the statue for victory, which, in a fashion, China gained. The statue was subsequently moved to the new temple built in Bangka (艋舺; today called Wanhua 萬華). This led to tension between adherents in the two communities.

It is said that in times of calamity or important events the statue's nose falls off.

The Qing-shui Zu-shi Temple in Sanhsia, noted for its fine carvings.

Guan Di
— *The Knights' Deity*

Sacrifice: 15th day of the 1st lunar month (1月15日)
Birthday: 24th day of the 6th lunar month (5月13日)

Guan Di (關帝; Emperor Guan or, according to one story, Emperor of the Pass) is one of the most popular deities in Taiwan. He is found commonly beside the ancestral tablet on family altars (where he faces the door, as "no evil spirit would dare to enter the presence of Guan Di") as well as in multi-deity temples and shrines (where he is easily picked out of the crowd by his red face). Moreover, he is not just worshiped on the first full moon of the New Year and his birthday, but also, as a patron deity of many trades, on a daily basis.

Furthermore, he is also one of that factions of historical figures worshiped as deities about whom much is known, or is thought to be known.

Fictional (and Factual) Hero

Even without his red face, Guan Di is recognizable by his beard and posture.

His story of bravery, honor, up-rightness and, ultimately, self-sacrifice is better known through the 14th-century novel *Romance of the Three Kingdoms* (三國演義) by Luo Guan-zhong (羅貫中) rather than the 4th-century *History of the Three Kingdoms* (三國誌) by Chen Shou (陳壽), on which it is based.

The story of the Epoch of the Three Kingdoms (220-265 CE) begins as the magnificent Han dynasty declines into chaos towards the end of the 2nd century CE; of particular importance is the rebellion in 184 by the Yellow Turbans (黃巾).

Two results of this are the rise of Cao Cao (曹操) from the status of minister to warlord contending for the throne of China, and the swearing in the Peach Garden of a brotherhood between Liu Bei (劉備), who shared

Temple mural showing Guan Yu with Liu Bei and Zhang Fei
declaring an oath of brotherhood in the Peach Garden.

the Han imperial surname, Zhang Fei (張飛), who is sometimes worshiped as the patron deity of butchers (because he
had been one), and Guan Yu (關羽), later deified as Guan Di.

In fact, there is some mystery surrounding Guan Yu's real
name (and his date of birth, though this is given tentatively as
165 CE). It may have been Yu (羽), Yun-chang (雲長) or
Zhang-sheng (長生), though these are usually offered as "style"
names, and he is said to have been born in what is today Jie
County (解縣) of Shanxi Province.

According to one version of his legend, Guan Yu was on the
run after having murdered a local official and his uncle, who
had tried to force his neighbor's daughter to become his
concubine. Blocked at a mountain pass, he is said to have
stopped to wash his face in a stream only to discover it had
turned red. Safe from recognition, when asked by the guards for
his name he replied Guan (關; pass).

Wooden carvings of Guan Di make popular souvenirs or statues for home shrines.

Chivalrous Knight and Protective Spirit

The brotherhood took part in many battles and their fame spread. Cao Cao, in particular, coveted his services but Guan Yu remained loyal to Liu Bei even after Cao had captured him. Later, having escaped and rejoined Liu, Guan Yu once spared Cao's life as he had been spared himself. This lead ultimately to his downfall.

Almost immediately after his death, invocation of his name is said to have been efficacious, and worship of his image to have exerted a benign influence on the nation's affairs. Initially he was posthumously entitled *Hou* (侯; Marquis), then worshiped as *Gong* (公; Duke), in the Song dynasty raised to Prince of Military Peace (武安王), and in the Ming to Loyal and Righteous Great Emperor who Assists Heaven and Defends the Nation (協天護國忠義大帝). He is also known by numerous other names, including simply Beautiful-Whiskered Duke (美髯公).

In English, it has become common to call him China's "God of War," but he in no way resembles the gods of war of other cultures' mythologies, and so is perhaps better described as the patron deity of knights. From this role, he was appropriated as patron deity by police, restaurants, the Qing emperors, as a god of wealth, a god of literature, and as the guardian of all brotherhoods and secret societies, and, therefore, ironically of criminals and rebels, against whom he first came to prominence.

Playing the Part

Actors portraying Guan Di in opera should never joke or chat in rehearsal, should abstain from meat and sex for ten days prior to performance (to make their bodies suitable vessels for his spirit), and should make offerings to his image before and after each show.

Guan Di is the main deity worshiped at Taipei's busy Xing Tian Temple.

Lord of the Land
—And Much, Much More

2nd day of the 2nd lunar month (2月2日)

Pilgrims to the Nan-shan Fu-de Temple in Zhonghe rub cash on *Tudi Gong*'s ingot to bring them prosperity in the coming year.

The main sacrifice to Lord of the Land (土地公) takes place on the 2nd day of the 2nd lunar month. One of the oldest and still one of the most widely worshiped deities in Taiwan, there are numerous temples dedicated to him throughout the main and offshore islands, as well as thousands, perhaps tens of thousands, of unregistered shrines found ubiquitously on roadsides and paddy fields. As one Taiwanese proverb says, "Lord of the Land [is worshiped] at both the top and bottom of a field" (*Chhan-tau chhan-bwey, Tho-ti-kong*).

Starting on the evening of the 1st, celebrations go on through most of the night, with faithful believers traveling long distances, often on foot, carrying palanquins bearing small statues of the deity from their own local shrine.

He is also worshiped as a god of wealth twice a month, when shopkeepers and others erect temporary altars outside their businesses, make offerings of food and drink, light incense and burn joss money.

Local (Spiritual) Official

Although the name *Tudi Gong* (土地公) is the official title of a member of the spiritual administration parallel to that of the emperor's government on earth, he is popularly worshiped as an individual. Indeed, he often represents the deification of a local person, whose protective powers are limited to that community. As another proverb says, "The God at the east end of the village is useless at the west."

Probably deriving from an ancient harvest festival or fertility worship, or from a combination of the Gods of Land and Millet (社稷), the simplest practices honoring *Tudi Gong* still often use merely a stone or tree, identified by a sash or inscription, rather than an image or deity statue.

When represented by a statue, he usually appears as a mild-faced, kindly elder with a long white beard, round cap and clothing of a country gentleman. Where someone passed the imperial examinations, he may wear an official's robes and hat. Sometimes he holds a long walking stick or a jade scepter (如意) in his right hand, and nothing or a gold ingot in his left hand. In mountainous regions, he may be portrayed riding on a tiger. Tigers are said to obey his commands, so he is also connected with the Lord Tiger (虎爺), found crouching beneath an altar in almost every temple.

Whatever his appearance and origins, *Tudi Gong's* main task is to look after the piece of land he governs. Therefore, whenever clearing new land, breaking the earth for sowing seed, or constructing or demolishing a house, grave or

Legendary Origins

According to one popular legend, Lord of the Land was the Minister of Agriculture under legendary Emperor Yao (堯; 2357-2255 BCE), who was worshiped because he taught people farming and animal husbandry.

Another story says he taught the people to plow the land and, after death, was enfeoffed by the City God as the "True Deity of Fortune and Virtue" (福德正神; Fu-de Zheng Shen).

Others say that he was originally a Zhou dynasty tax official named Zhang Fu-de, from which he got his title.

Incense and joss money are offered to Earth Governor (后土) beside a clan tomb.

Small shrines to Tudi Gong are found everywhere; this one is keeping watch over a farmer's field.

bridge, people make offerings to the Lord of the Land.

Naturally, he is of key importance in agricultural communities where harvest and prosperity depend on his assistance. In ancient times, as the nation's prosperity came to depend less on the land, he became a god of wealth (財神). As such, he is honored twice a month by both farmers (on the 1st and 15th of the lunar month) and business people (on the 2nd and 16th)*, when offerings are made at roadside altars.

Tudi Gong is also responsible for keeping records of all events occurring in the area under his jurisdiction, so announcements of births, marriages and deaths are usually made at his temple or shrine. In this capacity, he is similar to the City God of Walls and Moats (城隍爺), indeed, in urban areas, the latter seems to have usurped some of Tudi Gong's functions following urban development.

Stone statues of the Lord of the Land may resemble local figures.

"Making Tooth"

The bimonthly burning of joss money and making offerings is known as "making-tooth" (做牙) though the origin of this term is long-forgotten. Traditionally, bosses or heads of government departments also treated their workers to a meal, a habit now usually reserved for the last such day of each year, the "tail-tooth" (尾牙) on the 16th day of the 12th lunar month. As there are no "teeth made" during the New Year festivities, the 2nd day of the 2nd lunar month is the first such occasion, the "head-tooth" (頭牙). This, and the 15th day of the 8th month, are celebrated as *Tudi Gong's* official birthdays.

---

* Henri Maspero in *Taoism and Chinese Religion* suggests that this results from confusion between *Tudi Gong* in his role as God of Wealth, and the traditional twice-monthly offerings made to the God of Wealth who Increases Wealth.

Wenchang Di
— The Emperor of "Passing Exams"

3rd day of the 2nd lunar month (2月3日)

The birthday of Wenchang Di (文昌帝; Emperor of Prospering Culture) is celebrated on the 3rd day of the 2nd lunar month. This deity probably originated in the worship of a constellation of six stars, which was said to shine more brightly during periods when culture and literature flourished. Later he became the patron deity of scholars and literati, and, in addition to being represented by plaques, pictures or statues in shrines and temples, he is also found frequently in the homes and studies of educated Chinese.

Places to find him in Taipei include Longshan Temple, Bao-an Temple and Xing Tian Temple among many others.

Photocopies of student IDs are left before Wenchang Di's statue by devout (or perhaps desperate) students.

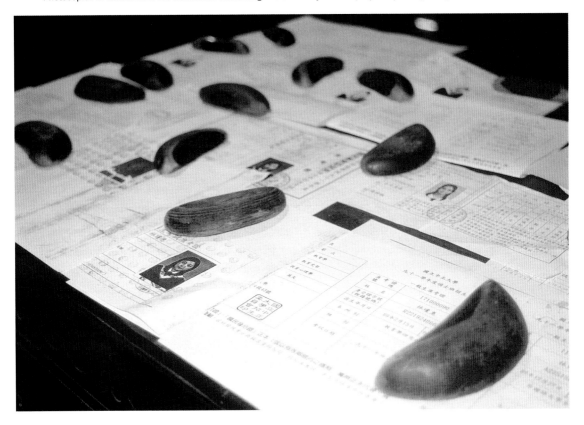

Tomb-Sweeping Festival
— Brooms, Cold Foods and Paradoxes

April 5th (international calendar)

Before and after tomb-sweeping.

The "Bright and Clear Festival" (清明節), popularly known as Tomb-Sweeping Festival (掃墓節), which now takes place annually on April 5th, is one of very few of Taiwan's traditional cultural and religious events to follow the international solar calendar rather than the Chinese lunar one. This is especially surprising since this festival dates back at least two millennia.

Another surprise is that although everyone in Taipei knows that, as well as tidying the family grave, it is traditional to eat lumpia (潤餅) "Chinese pancakes," most people have forgotten the reason.

Ancestor Worship

Perhaps because of its connection with the arrival of spring, the *qingming* (清明) period (one of the twenty-four solar terms 節氣 of the supplementary "farmers'" calendar) became gradually associated with cleaning and maintaining one's family grave, and making formal sacrifices to one's ancestors.

The importance of graves, spirits and ancestral worship is central to Chinese religiosity and, by at least the Eastern Han dynasty (25-220 CE), the imperial household held annual ceremonies on fixed dates, not just to worship their ancestors but also to renovate the gravesites. This was held most frequently in the first lunar month, but varied from dynasty to dynasty and even from emperor to emperor. In the Tang dynasty, the imperial court fixed the "Cold Food Festival" (寒食節) as the correct occasion on which to "climb the hill and worship at the tomb." An edict was also passed allowing the common people to make similar sacrifices to their own ancestors and to clean graves on this day. During the Ming dynasty, this was changed slightly to the qingming day. In addition, a second ceremony was established on the full moon of the seventh lunar month (which is now celebrated as the Pu-du 普渡 festival of ghost month).

Cold Food Festival

Duke Xian (獻公), ruler of the small state of Jin (晉) during the Epoch of Spring and Autumn (770-403 BCE) in what are parts of today's Shanxi and Hebei provinces, influenced by his favorite secondary wife, proclaimed her son as his successor. He also ordered the three sons by his first wife to be killed.

Before his orders could be carried out, his eldest son killed himself in an act of filial piety, while the younger two fled led into exile.

Over the next nineteen years, the elder of these, Chong-er (重耳, whose name seems to mean "Double Ears") saw a fluctuation in his fortunes. On one occasion, when he faced starvation, his loyal official Jie Zhi-tui (介之推) cut flesh from his own thigh, which he cooked and fed to his master.

After returning to Jin and assuming the throne as Duke Wen (文; Civilizer), Chong-er rewarded those ministers who had remained with him through the bad times. Somehow he overlooked Jie's incomparable sacrifice.

Jie, meanwhile, turned his back on official life and retired to live with his mother in a mountain forest.

Alerted to his oversight, Duke Wen quickly sent people to track down Jie, but the latter preferred his hermit's life. Someone then suggested setting fire to the mountain so that Jie, as a filial son, was sure to come rushing down bearing his mother on his back. The ensuing fire raged for three days and nights, but still Jie Zhi-tui did not appear.

After the fire had burnt itself out, Jie and his mother's bodies were found deep in the forest, their arms wrapped around a willow tree.

Consumed by remorse, Duke Wen ordered the mountain renamed Mount Jie and had a shrine built honoring the two victims. Each year on this day, people show their respect by placing willow branches outside their homes (other trees are used in Taiwan where willows are scarce), and Duke Wen ordered that no one should use fire, designating it Cold Food Day.

Lumpia are still eaten in memory of Jie Zhi-tui, who burnt to death two-and-a-half millennia ago.

Taiwanese Import

In the Quanzhou (泉州) Prefecture of Fujian Province, it became the practice to clean graves "at least by" the *qingming* day, for which an auspicious day was selected according to the almanac. Around Zhangzhou (漳州), it was generally performed on *qingming* itself. These two practices were brought to Taiwan by the early immigrants, laying the basis for today's ceremonies.

Nowadays, descendents of both groups tend to visit clan graves on qingming itself, making it a national celebration. Since grave sites with good *feng-shui* are scarce, and since many graveyards are in the suburbs or in the rural hometowns of Taipei's economic migrants, Tomb-Sweeping Day often becomes an excuse for a family get-together and excursion, known traditionally as "treading on green [grass]" (踏青). Many Overseas Chinese time their annual visit home to coincide with this event as an expression of filial piety and clan identity.

How to Tomb-Sweep

Tomb-sweeping activities can be divided into three parts: grave maintenance, "hanging paper" (掛紙) and worship.

"Banking up the tomb with earth" (培墓), is the somewhat antiquated but descriptive name for maintaining the grave, since it may require some more extensive work on the soil and brickwork. Tomb inscriptions may be retouched with gold or red paint.

When the grave is acceptably tidy, it is covered with sheets of ghost money or colored paper, held

Family members take it in turns to offer prayers to their ancestors.

down by small stones. This "hanging grave paper" is not for decoration but, as on other occasions when joss paper is burnt, to provide one's ancestors with money to spend in the nether world.

Spirit money is also pinned onto a small "tombstone" at the side of the main grave. Inscribed "Earth Governor" (后土), this is a plaque for offerings to the "Lord of the Land" (土地公), who oversees a community's births and deaths, among other duties.

Prayer

The family now make offerings of food and drink, incense is lit, carrying prayers and good wishes towards the heavens, and firecrackers might be let off, to prevent hungry ghosts, who do not have filial descendants, from gate-crashing the occasion.

Father, mother, sons then daughters, bow in turn before the grave and offer prayers. The prayers offered depend on the beliefs of the individual, Confucian, Buddhist, Daoist or even Christian. The willingness of some Christian sects proselytizing in China to tolerate ancestor worship led to intense debate and worse with other missionary groups.

In a practice that dates back to pre-Confucian times, at least one glass of alcohol is poured onto the ground to share with local spirits, a habit some people maintain anytime they open a new bottle.

Traditional food offerings include meat, wine, noodles and "red turtle cakes" (紅龜粿) which were handed out to nearby cattle-herding children, perhaps to bribe them not to let their charges wander and defecate over the graves. This practice has largely disappeared, though some people pass out money to local children.

Once the ancestral spirits have eaten their fill, the offerings may be eaten by the family or taken home.

Today, the most characteristic food eaten on Tomb-Sweeping Day is lumpia (*run-bing* in Mandarin), Chinese pancake-style snacks filled with cold meat, vegetables, bean sprouts and peanut paste wrapped in a thin wheat skin. Deriving from the customs of Cold Food Day commemorating Jie Zhi-tui, the two festivals, originally separated by one day, have now become confused and inseparable in popular practice.

Hanging Paper Legend

According to one legend, the practice of pinning paper to graves is said to have started with the first emperor of the Tang dynasty. He had been so busy establishing the dynasty that by the time he returned to his hometown, his mother had already died. Distraught at his unfilial behavior, he tried to make good her needs in the next life.

"Hanging paper" is an important task once the grave has been tidied and renovated.

Bao-sheng Da-Di
—*The Great Emperor Who Preserves Life*

15th day of the 3rd lunar month (3月15日)

With everyone spilling out of their homes to fill the narrow cobbled lanes, the birthday of "The Great Emperor Who Preserves Life"(保生大帝) is the highlight of the year for this community in Taipei's Dalongtong district (大龍峒).

Located next-door to the Confucius Temple (孔子廟), the two-hundred-year-old Bao-an Temple (保安宮) creates an ideal atmosphere for a traditional birthday celebration.

The deity's mix of historical fact and mythical story is also typical of the process by which, after death, the spirit of a local hero becomes the focus of people's prayers and offerings. As his or her fame spreads, some may gain official patronage or may even be promoted to the ranks of the Daoist pantheon.

Food fights break out as spectators scramble for lucky buns.

The History...

Born on the 15th day of the 3rd lunar month of 979 CE (during the Song dynasty) in Tongan County (同安縣) in Quanzhou Prefecture (泉州) in Fujian Province, he was originally named Wu Tao (吳　). He is said to have been a precocious child, learning quickly and memorizing lengthy classical texts. He passed the civil examinations and served as Imperial Censor (御史), before retiring, changing his name to Hua Zhi (華枝; Flowering Branch), and dedicating himself to the study of medicine and helping others. He never married and did not eat meat.

He first gained public attention in 1032 when, during a great famine throughout Quanzhou, he predicted the arrival of grain supplies. The next year, he is said to have provided the cure for a terrible epidemic. He died in 1037 at the age of 58.

Bao-sheng Da-di, once a retired official of the Song dynasty, is now worshiped as a medical deity.

...and Legend

Whilst the date of his birth is agreed upon, its manner is contested. Various legends circulate, the most common being his was an immaculate conception resulting from his mother's dream in which she swallowed a white turtle.

His healing skills are said to have come from the mystical arts of the Queen Mother of the West (西王母) rather than through a lifetime of study. Among his numerous acts of compassion, he is said to have resurrected a dead child from a pile of dry bones. Legends agree that he was "commanded to heaven by the Jade Emperor" in 1037.

Talismans are pasted to the deity's palanquin to protect him across the fire.

After his death, people of his home village built a temple in his honor, venerating him as "True Gentleman Wu" (吳真君). Even from the spirit world he is said to have continued to perform miracles and help people. Most noticeably, Wu is said to have taken on the form of a Daoist priest to cure the wife of Ming emperor Cheng-zu (成祖; r. 1403-1424) of breast cancer, reading her pulses from the next room by means of strings. In gratitude, the emperor ordered a new, grander temple to be built and entitled him "Everlasting and Limitless Great Emperor Who Preserves Life."

Journey to Taiwan

Statues of this deity were first brought to Taiwan in the middle of the 17th century when the Dutch settlers encouraged Chinese from Quanzhou and Zhangzhou (漳州) prefectures in Fujian Province to emigrate to Taiwan.

Protected by deities' statues and joss money, this participant is ready to "run the fiery coals."

There are now more than two hundred temples dedicated to the "Heavenly Doctor" throughout the island, including Taipei's at 61 HaMi Street (哈密街). Dating from 1805, it is located in what then was the flourishing business district near the junction of the Danshui and Keelung rivers.

The main hall dedicated to Bao-sheng Da-di established with incense brought from Tongan and numerous smaller side "chapels" took a quarter-century to complete. Stone and timber used in its construction and ornamentation came from mainland China, as did the artisans. It is one of the city's finest examples of temple architecture and has been repaired frequently over the last two centuries.

Party of the Year

The weeklong birthday celebrations are also among the city's best, including operatic and other performances, art and photography competitions, a day-long street parade, lion dancing, and a ritual fire-walking ceremony.

The street parade has many of the usual figures, including the God of Wealth (財神), Lord of the Land (土地公), giant human-occupied puppets of Seventh Lord (七爺) and Eighth Lord (八爺), as well as the usual melange of raucous pipe music, teams of drummers and strings of firecrackers ignited each time a deity in a palanquin is carried up to the censer in front of the temple's main door to make pay homage to Bao-sheng Da-di.

Unusual appearances include girls dressed as boys, men dressed as women, people dressed as cows and horses, the "Divine Farmer" (Shen Nong; 神農), the Twelve Maternal Ancestors (十二婆祖) who assist with childbirth in each of the twelve months, a performance of kung-fu by stilt-walking mythological figures, and giant figures mobbed by the public trying to grab bread rolls strung about their necks supposed to bring good fortune. This wider-than-normal range of deities reflects the eclectic collection of deities inhabiting the temple's lesser chapels and which makes this one of Taipei's best temples to visit at any time.

The final day begins with the formality of a Confucian-style ceremony befitting someone elevated to imperial status by the emperor of China himself. In the afternoon, a huge pile of charcoal is lit, becoming so hot that spectators are driven back to the corners of the courtyard. Broken into pieces, raked flat and then covered with salt, the twenty-meter course is ready. A Daoist priest makes offerings of food and wine to benign spirits and beats the ground to drive off malevolent ones, and then is the first to run across the coals, followed by pairs of men fulfilling a vow or seeking spiritual merit by carrying statues tied to palanquins across the hot surface.

Locals have great fun dressing up; these gentlemen have come as the temple's Twelve Maternal Ancestors.

Stilt performers recount classical tales in front of the Bao-an Temple's main doors.

Ms. Lin
—Maternal Ancestor and Queen of Heaven

23rd day of the 3rd lunar month (3 月 23 日)

Destined to become one of Taiwan's most popular religious figures, Lin Mo (林默) was probably born in 960 CE on the island of Meizhou (湄州嶼) off the coast of Fujian Province, a distant outpost of the Song dynasty. It is said she was given the name Mo (默; silent) as she rarely cried as a baby.

Her life thereafter is an inextricable mix of history (very few details are listed in records of the Song dynasty) and mythology. She was either the daughter of a fisherman or lowly official. Apparently, although her parents were devout Buddhist worshipers of Guanyin (觀音), when aged thirteen, Ms. Lin was identified as being an extraordinary person by a Daoist priest, who then taught her his mystical arts. At sixteen, she is said to have discovered an immortal's pair of bronze talismans (銅符), which helped her keep evil at bay and protect life. She died in 987 at the age of 28, having refused all offers of marriage.

Mazu, Queen of Heaven, is one of Taiwan's most popular deities.

"Ears that Hear on the Wind" and "Thousand-Mile Eyes" are Mazu's assistants in saving imperiled seafarers.

Savior of Seafarers

She is said to have saved her father (or possibly brothers) from drowning, possibly during a dream or trance. One version of the story recounts that in the middle of her fit, she was woken by her mother, upon which she reprimanded her mother, saying she had been brought back too soon and, while her brother was saved, her father was lost.

After her death she continued to save other imperiled seafarers, often through miraculous acts, for which became worshiped as Mazu (媽祖; Maternal Ancestor).

By saving an imperial official traveling to Korea in 1122 she came to the attention of the court and was quickly promoted to Supernatural Princess, Queen, Holy Queen (聖母), and finally in 1278, to Queen of Heaven (天后). It is said that this latter, most surprising, promotion, at the beginning of the Yuan dynasty may have been a diplomatic move by the new Mongol dynasty to ensure allegiance by coastal peoples on the edge of their new empire.

Other scholars suggest that her rapid promotion within Daoism was because of the increasing popularity of the Buddhist figure Guanyin , also characterized by compassion and salvation.

Mazu's Eyes and Ears

In Taipei's temples, Mazu is usually seen flanked by two striking figures: "Ears that Hear on the Wind" (順風耳) and "Thousand-Mile Eyes" (千里眼). Legend tells that these two demons, like so many hapless suitors, fell in love with Mazu but, having been converted to her spiritual path, they now assist her in locating sailors in trouble.

Whatever the cause, Mazu's popularity along the Chinese coastline meant that she traveled with the first immigrants to Taiwan. Today there are more than four hundred temples dedicated to Mazu throughout Taiwan.

Pilgrims and Partygoers

Mazu's temples bear a variety of titles such as Holy Mother of Heaven (天上聖母) or Queen of Heaven. Taiwan's oldest is at Makung in the Penghu Islands; the most famous is at Dachia near Taichung. In annual rituals dating back at least 150 years, devotees carry effigies to satellite temples in neighboring districts, "sharing holy incense" (分香) and bringing spiritual salvation to each community. Pilgrims, including many fulfilling vows, make the journey to Mazu's original home in Fujian Province across the Taiwan Strait.

Many temples dedicated to some other deity will also have an altar or statue in Mazu's name and will celebrate her birthday.

The enormous popularity of Mazu's birthday celebrations suggest that although most Taiwanese long ago exchanged this reliance on the sea for a livelihood of manufacturing and trade, this fisherman's daughter has retained her place in their hearts.

Joss money is thrown in the air as the Eight Generals (八家將) perform in front of the Ci-You Temple on Mazu's birthday.

Cleansing the Buddha Festival

8th day of the 4th lunar month (4月8日)

In accordance with Indian customs, Lady Maya, heavy with child, was traveling back to her parents' home to give birth. She paused for a rest in Lumbini Park near Vapilavastu in northern India (today, just over the border in Nepal) and, grasping a branch of the *asoka* (without sorrow) tree, gave birth. Her son, named Siddhartha Gautama, would become the historical Buddha Śākyamuni (Sage of the Śakya clan).

Buddhist legend now claims that Buddha's father, Suddhodana, was ruler of the Sakya state, that Siddhartha appeared from the right side of his mother's torso rather than the normal route of childbirth, that he appeared as an infant rather than baby, and immediately took "seven steps in the four directions," pointed one hand upwards towards heaven and the other down towards the ground, and proclaimed, "Whether above or below heaven, I am most noble and high. I am here to bring peace to all the sentient beings in the world who are suffering." He was then sprinkled with scented water by the nine dragons of heaven.

Whatever the truth, it is this last part of the story that is reenacted each year in the Cleansing Buddha Festival (浴佛節).

Temple decoration depicting the dragons of heaven spitting water towards earth.

Lost in Time

Despite being a historical figure, the date of the Buddha's birth is uncertain. In Taiwan's Mahayana Buddhist community, this is celebrated on the 8th day of the 4th lunar month; among Theravada communities, it is celebrated between April 10th and April 18th, which is known as *Sonkran* in Thailand (see below).

Even the year of the birth of Siddhartha (One who has achieved his aim) is the focus of much debate between the different Buddhist traditions. Using ancient Sri Lankan chronicles, the southern Theravada (Teachings of the Elders) school dates his life to 566-486 BCE, so that the year 2000 was celebrated as 2542 in Thailand, from the year of his enlightenment. The northern Mahayana (Greater Vehicle) school places his birth some two hundred years later. Recent archaeological evidence also leans towards a later date, suggesting his birth may have been in the late 5th or early 4th century BCE.

Theravada Buddhist monks officiate at the Songkran Festival in Nanshijiao.

Statue of Buddha in the Theravada style protected from the sun by symbolic parasols.

Birthday Celebrations

In today's Taipei, there are three main ways in which the Buddha's birth is celebrated: Lantern lighting (點燈), Cleansing Buddha Festival (浴佛節), and Sonkran (known in Chinese as 潑水節; Water-Sprinkling Festival).

Lantern lighting perhaps originates in the Buddhist story of a lantern lit by a poor woman, which could not be extinguished because it had been lit with great devotion and sincerity.

The Cleansing Buddha Festival, which is said to imitate the celestial dragons welcoming Siddhartha into the world, may have an even older origin, perhaps deriving from the ancient Indian custom of anointing kings with water from the rivers in his kingdom, from a religious baptism, or simply from the washing of all newborn children.

This ceremony was popular throughout the period of Japanese rule (1895-1945) despite the promulgation of Shinto as state religion, and was generally held in the Taihoku Park (today, the 2-28 Memorial Park). It fell from favor after Taiwan's retrocession in 1945, being kept alive privately at a few temples. It is now growing in popularity once more.

A devout worshiper in traditional costume.

Statues of the infant Buddha are erected beneath a bower of flowers representing the blossoms in the park at Lumbini. After the temple's abbot or head monk has poured water over the Buddha's head, other monks, nuns and lay Buddhists do the same in strict order. Throughout this time, the gathered believers recite sutras, chant mantras and bang gongs. In addition to congratulating the Buddha on his birthday, participants also reconfirm their "refuge in the three treasures of Buddhism," that is, in the Buddha as teacher, *dharma* natural law and *sangha* monastic community (佛、法、僧).

People take home some of the "nectar" that runs off to drink later. This scented water is made with incense constituents such as aloeswood (沉香), sandalwood (白檀), sweet pine (甘松), *Cnidium officinale* (芎藭), and *Curcuma longa* (鬱金). Lotus flowers are also in profusion as they represent the highest purity of Buddhism; just as this ceremony represents the ritual cleansing of one's passions, greed and egoism, the impurities of the human realm.

Good places to participate include Longshan Temple (龍山寺) in Wanhua and Nungchan Temple (農禪寺) in Peitou.

Cleansing Buddha, Drenching Everyone —
The "Water-sprinkling Festival" Thai-style in Nanshijiao

Nanshijiao (南勢角) at the end of the Chungho MRT line is home to Taiwan's largest population of Overseas Chinese originating from Southeast Asia. Particularly famed for the quantity and variety of Myanmar, Thai and Yunnan restaurants, HuaXin St. (華新街) is known throughout Taipei as "Burma Street" (緬甸街) after the ten thousand local people who arrived in Taiwan from Myanmar.

Although Han-Chinese, having lived among Theravada Buddhists speaking different languages and practicing different customs, this part of Taipei has its own unique culture, cuisine, *lingua franca*, religious practices and even its own way of celebrating the Buddha's birthday.

For one thing they do it on a different day, the day when the sun passes from Aries to Taurus, a date known as *Sonkran* in Thailand, and which falls between April 10th and April 18th, marking the Thai New Year.

The refined custom of pouring water over statues of the infant Buddha is replaced by a full-scale battle in which buckets of water are thrown over willing adversaries and innocent bystanders alike. Instead of taking the water run-off home to quench one's bodily and spiritual thirst, the Theravada practice is to sprinkle a little over the shoulder of an elderly person as a sign of respect and to wish them good fortune in the year ahead. In return, a string similarly representing good luck is tied around the sprinkler's wrist.

Somehow this sprinkling has evolved into today's practice of throwing water over everyone in sight.

Water-sprinkling evolved gradually into today's full-scale water fights.

Unkillable Demon — Legend of the Dai People

The Dai ethnic group of Yunnan in southwestern China has an alternative explanation of the origins of the Water-Sprinkling Festival, which they have carried with them since leaving their homelands further east in southern China.

They recount that in these ancient homelands there was a demon king, so evil that the common people's suffering was unendurable. He stole their money and had taken six women to become his wives. Moreover, he seemed impervious to fire and even to drowning. One day he captured an intelligent and beautiful maiden for his seventh bride. This woman resolved to rid the people of their suffering.

Waiting until the demon king was drunk, she tricked him into revealing that he could be killed only by using a strand of his own hair. The maiden therefore plucked a hair from the demon's head, garroted him with it and watched his head fall to the ground.

Unfortunately, the demon's head was still able to harm people. When the seven wives tried to burn it, the human world was consumed by fire; when they buried it, the stench became unbearable; when they threw it in the river, the river boiled up and flooded.

Left with no alternative, the seven women took turns to hold up the head so that it never touched the ground. Each turn lasted one year and, at the hand-over, pure water was used to wash the head of its evil and the women of their bloodstains.

Retelling of this story forms part of the Dai's New Year festivities.

The Extreme Yang of Summer
—And the Dragon Boat Festival

5th day of the 5th lunar month (5 月 5 日)

Surprisingly, in a calendar year filled with religious celebrations, the three major festivals (三節) are largely secular, centering around gatherings of family and friends, delicacies of food and drink, and theatrical performances and impromptu composition of poetry.

Religious aspects and origins are often present but less obvious, especially to the outsider.

"Highest Noon" Festival

Chinese tend to speak of the "Highest Noon" (端午節) or "Extreme *Yang*" (端陽節) festival rather than Dragon Boat Festival. One origin, therefore, derives from a midsummer festival when the sun was at its highest and the heats of summer started to become oppressive and to bring with them threatening pestilences. Too much *yang* (the element of the sun and summer), just as too much *yin* (shade and winter), was considered unhealthy and dangerous. This was symbolized by the "five noxious creatures" (五毒), which were the centipede, scorpion , snake, lizard and toad, (other lists include wasps, spiders and so forth)

To protect themselves from these, and the unseen evil spirits that accompanied them, people carried or wore sprigs of calamus and mugwort. These plants can still be seen in Taipei at this time

Dragon boat racing demonstrates the Chinese virtues of teamwork and cooperation. (Photo by Wang Neng-yu)

of year, usually tied to doors and gateways. *Xiong-huang Jiu* (雄黃酒), wine containing realgar, an arsenic sulfide originally used in firework manufacture, is also drunk as a protective medicine. Pictures of Zhong Kui (鍾馗) the champion demon-slayer are hung up.

Zhong Kui the Exorcist

There are various myths connected with Zhong Kui, most of which portray him as a poor and unsuccessful scholar, who returned to the human realm after his death to help quell demons.

One version tells that he was a physician from Shaanxi (陝西) Province, who failed the public examinations so often he could only become a doctor or teacher. Believing that corrupt officials had cheated him of his rightful position, he committed suicide on the imperial palace steps.

Later, after the Tang emperor Xuan Zong (唐玄宗; r. 713-756) in a fever dreamt he was cured by the ghost of Zhong Kui, the latter's body was exhumed and reburied with full rights and given the title Great Spiritual Chaser of Demons for the Whole Empire.

One other explanation is that he is the personification of a plant 終葵, similarly pronounced *zhong-kui,* which had magical properties warding off evil spirits.

Calamus and mugwort are hung on doors to keep the Five Noxious Creatures away.

A local dignitary dots the dragon's eyes, "bringing it to life."

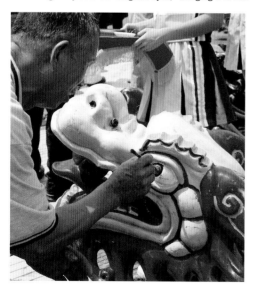

Ministry of Exorcisms

Less-frequently depicted, but having even greater status in the heavenly "Ministry of Exorcisms," is Zhang Dao-ling (張道陵), first patriarch of the School of Heavenly Masters (天師派), who had the greatest influence on formulating Daoism as a formal religion.

To perform an exorcism, priests armed with fans, scrolls and peachwood swords combat the demons responsible. They also pin up talismans, sprinkle cockerel's blood and chant incantations.

Dragon boat racing—encouraging fertility,
exorcising evil or just fun and games.

Buddhist monks recite blessings before
the dragon boat races begin.

Drowned Poet Society

The best-known story concerning the Dragon Boat Festival is that of Qu Yuan (屈原; 340?-278 BCE), poet and statesman of Chu (楚) during the Epoch of Warring States (475-221 BCE). His talents became the target of envy and slander, and his achievements were claimed by others. In response, Qu composed his most famous poem "Encountering Sorrow" (離騷), whose hero, slandered by political enemies and dismissed from court, undertakes a mystical journey in search of a virtuous ruler. The poem ends ambiguously, leaving the reader to decide whether the hero will return to his homeland, continue his search, retire as a hermit, or commit suicide.

Eventually, Qu himself weighed down his robes with stones and threw himself into the Milo River (汨羅江). This is said to have occurred on the fifth day of the fifth month.

Legend recounts that fishermen rushed to their boats in an attempt to save him (supposedly, the origin of today's dragon boat races), then threw rice into the river to prevent fish eating his corpse (the origin of the *zong-zi* 粽子 rice tamales eaten today).

Before the races, local dignitaries including politicians from the Taipei City Government take part in an "eye-dotting ceremony" to paint the dragon boats' eyes in auspicious red, bringing them alive. Daoist priests or Buddhist monks hold religious ceremonies on the shore, then the rowers paddle up and down, throwing joss money into the water in memory of Qu, and letting off firecrackers.

Sacrifices to Dragons

The act of making offerings (including unmarried girls) to water dragons and spirits, is probably much older and represented ancient attempts to control the flooding and droughts of China's many rivers.

Dragon boat competitors throw joss money
into the river before competition begins.

Cheng-Huang Ye
— the Lord of Walls and Moats

13th day of the 5th lunar month (5月13日)-Xia-Hai Temple
25th October (International Calendar)-Provincial City God Temple

More commonly known simply as the "City God," the Lord of Walls and Moats (城隍爺) is a curious mixture of history and myth. On the one hand he represents heaven's authority on earth, keeping records of important events such as births and deaths, and of the moral behavior of the citizens. On the other hand, he often commemorates a local worthy, whose divine protection, the people of a town or city wish to perpetuate.

Perhaps it is because of this, that the City God's birthday is celebrated on different days in different regions of Taiwan. These include Tainan on 4/20, Makung on 5/6, Miaoli on 5/11, Chiayi on 5/28, Changhua on 6/13, and Taichung and Nantou on 6/15.

At Taipei's Xia-hai Temple (霞海城隍廟) at No.61, DiHua Street (迪化街), he is honored on the 13th day of the 5th lunar month; and on Retrocession Day (October 25th) at the Taiwan Provincial City God Temple (台灣省城隍廟) at 14 WuChang Street (武昌街). The former is set in a rather sleepy street in the heart of Taipei's historic Dadaocheng (大稻埕) district, with its herbal suppliers and barrel makers, bursts into life twice a year.

The first occasion is Chinese New Year when the famous DiHua Street Market sells everything needed for the festive season, from dried persimmon and mullet roe, to spring couplets and wealth-Beckoning cats (招財貓). The second is City God's birthday, when once more the street comes alive, but this time with fireworks and giant marionettes.

Statue of the City God is brought to the main doors to receive worshipers' birthday wishes.

This traditional plaque reads "You too will come" (你也來了) reminding visitors to the Provincial City God Temple that one day they will be judged for their actions.

Parallel Administration

Festivities start a couple of evenings earlier, when the statues of deities from neighboring temples are carried by palanquin on the shoulders of adherents to pay their respects to the birthday deity. Pipes are blown, gongs beaten, firecrackers ignited and joss money thrown into the air. Representatives of the temples also dress up as the City God and his attendants.

In a parallel administration to that of the local yamen (衙門; the traditional local government), the City God has a complex department of subordinates to help him. These include Judge Wen (文判官) and Judge Wu (武判官), mirroring the civil (文) and military (武) division of the emperor's earthly regime; Lord Ox (牛爺) and Lord Horse (馬爺), the Officials of Yin and Yang, and, particularly eye-catching in their giant costumes as they parade down DiHua Street, Seventh Lord (七爺) and Eighth Lord (八爺).

Seventh Lord and Eighth Lord

There are various versions of the story of the Seventh Lord and Eighth Lord, the most common being that they were two generals and devoted friends. One day, they arranged to meet beneath a bridge spanning a river, but unfortunately the rains were heavy and the waters rose. Furthermore, General Xie Bi-an (謝必安-later known as the Seventh Lord) was delayed, but General Fan Wu-jiu (范無救; Eighth Lord), determined to keep the appointment, remained beneath the bridge and drowned. Finally turning up, General Xie was so filled with remorse that he hung himself from the bridge.

The Seventh Lord can therefore be recognized by his long and protruding tongue (a result of hanging himself by the neck), tall stature (he is nicknamed Chang Ye 長爺; Lanky Lord), tall hat on which is written, "Immense good fortune on first sight" (一見大吉), the fan in his right hand, and implements of torture in his left with which he subdues evil spirits in the course of his work.

The Eighth Lord has a blackened face (a result of drowning), short stature (he is nicknamed Duan Ye 短爺; Little Lord), low hat on which is written, "Become rich on first sight" (一見發財), the fire tablet held in his left hand and chain in his right, and his staring eyes as he goes about his administrative duties.

Seventh "Lanky" Lord has a long tongue, resulting from death by hanging.

Eighth "Little" Lord is portrayed with his face blackened through drowning.

The City God and his assistants judge the spirits of the dead in the courts of hell, rewarding benevolence and punishing wickedness. The Seventh and Eighth Lords help capture evil spirits and keep an eye on living people's behavior.

People pray to the City God for protection and prosperity, for rain after drought and sun after thunderstorms. They report the community's births and deaths to him, and in this role he resembles an urban version of Lord of the Land (土地公; *Tudi Gong*), an older deity dating from when people's livelihood was closely bound to the fertility of the land.

The emergence of the City God is connected to China's urbanization, particularly during the Tang dynasty. Cheng-Huang Ye's name hints towards his early duties: *cheng* (城) refers to the protective city wall and *huang* (隍) to the dry moat outside the wall. The "Lord of Wall and Moat" therefore represented early city dwellers' hopes and fears within their fortified homes.

Bodhisattva Guanyin
— Hearer of the World's Cries

19th day of the 6th lunar month (6月19日)

Statue of the bodhisattva Guanyin as (s)he appears in Taipei's Da-An Park.

Guanyin, who celebrates her Attainment of the Way (得道) on the 13th day of the 6th month, typifies the complicated process by which a Buddhist figure is transformed, firstly to fit the ideals of Chinese Buddhist schools, then further as she is adopted by popular religious practices.

Ideal of Compassion

Originating in Indian Buddhism as a man and known as the bodhisattva Avalokiteśvara, he most probably represented the ideal of consummate compassion rather than being a historical figure (though some scholars suggest he might have entered Indian Buddhism from local Iranian beliefs to the northwest; from an indigenous Indian deity who protected against smallpox; or via Sri Lanka from south Arabian seamen).

A bodhisattva is a "being whose essence is wisdom," but who has renounced their personal liberation and Nirvana in order to help save all other "sentient beings." Although not unknown in southern Theravada Buddhism, expansion of their key role is central to the Mahayana Buddhism of China, Tibet and Japan. Indeed, this is the origin of the name Mahayana, which means "greater vehicle," that is, Buddhism for the salvation of all, and all monks and nuns of the Chinese schools take a Vow of the Bodhisattva.

In his compassionate vow to "ferry beings across the sea of suffering to the other shore (Nirvana)," Avalokiteśvara is counterpart to Manjusri (*Wenshu;* 文殊), the bodhisattva of wisdom.

Salvation through Faith

Emergence of Avalokiteśvara, reaching out to any being who calls his name, represented a new devotional cult within Buddhism. Indeed, in Chinese Buddhism, the bodhisattva Guanyin is often

Guanyin is so popular she pops up in all manner of Buddhist and Daoist temples.

associated with the Amitha Buddha, whose Pureland in the west is open to anyone who recites his name, not merely those that attain *bodhi* wisdom through spiritual practice, the abnegation of self, and enlightenment to their own buddha-nature.

This is expressed in the *Lotus Sutra* (妙法蓮華經), which introduces Guanyin:

"If there be any who hold fast to the name of that bodhisattva, Regarder-of-Cries, though they fall in a great fire, the fire will not be able to burn them... if any, carried away by flood, call upon his name, they will immediately reach the shallows..."*

As the translator, W.E. Soothill, points out, this represents a complete reversal of the Buddha's earlier teaching.

The bodhisattva Guanyin is the main "deity" worshiped at Taipei's popular Longshan Temple.

* *Lotus Sutra,* trans. W.E. Soothill

The Chinese name, Guanyin meaning "Regarder of Cries," is a rare example of a Buddhist name being translated rather than merely transliterated. Unfortunately, there has always been debate over the real meaning of the Sanskrit Avalokiteśvara, however, as to whether the last part is *svara* (sounds) or, more likely, *isvara* (sovereign). Following the latter interpretation, his name is also translated as Guan-zizai (觀自在; Self-existent Regarder).

Gender Crossing

Harder to explain is Avalokiteśvara's transformation from male bodhisattva to female deity.

One reason might be that the thirty-two physiological signs of any enlightened figure include such female-like attributes as slender fingers, soft skin, long eyelashes and even a retracted penis. Early Buddhist art also shows Avalokiteśvara with gentle facial features and well-developed chest muscles. In crossing political, ethnic and linguistic borders, it would have been easy to mistake his appearance as that of a woman.

Guanyin is said to hear, and respond to, appeals for help from anyone.

Alternatively, to meet the challenge of Daoism in China, it was useful for Buddhism to have a feminine figure of similar status to that of Mazu, the Daoist Goddess of Mercy (though others claim the opposite, that Mazu's promotion was to complement Guanyin in Buddhism).

Some people offer as explanation the natural association of mercy and compassion with women in the Chinese mind.

In fact, none of these explanations is necessary as, like other enlightened beings, Avalokiteśvara is capable of a thousand different emanations for each of the thousand worlds in the universe. He (or she) appears in whatever form is expedient for saving the beings of that world. This is depicted artistically in the thousand-arm thousand-eye statues of Guanyin.

Whatever the explanation, it is fitting there is a female deity at the center of Taipei religious worship since women form the backbone of all the city's religious practice.

Pu-Du (Universal Ferry) — *Feeding the "Good Brothers"*

15th day of the 7th lunar month (7月15日)

On the first day of the seventh lunar month, the gates of hell are opened (鬼門開) allowing ghosts to wander the earth. They are not closed (鬼門關) again until the last day of the month, 29½ days later. In the meantime, many local people will refrain from various activities and make lavish offerings to placate any mischievous ghosts.

People will rarely open a new business in this month, or plant crops, move home, rearrange furniture, erect a stove or marry. Superstitious people will also travel less, and will avoid leaving clothes outside overnight, in case they are worn by ghosts, which might lead to illness or death of the owner. Some people will not go out after dark, and almost no one will go swimming.

Drownings and Suicides

The disinclination to go swimming, even though the weather is usually hot, results from Chinese people's ideas about death. In brief, a person whose descendents carry out the appropriate funeral ceremonies and make regular offerings will become an ancestral spirit (神); those whose "sons and grandsons" neglect their duties becomes a ghost (鬼) and suffers torment in the afterlife. People dying far from home, without an heir, and by drowning or suicide, also become ghosts. Let out from hell, they seek substitute bodies with which to continue their own transmigration (rebirth), and swimmers present easy targets. It is said that people are loath to save a drowning person in case they are taken instead.

Normal food, which may be offered to spirits, is said to turn to fire on the lips of these "hungry ghosts," also known euphemistically as "good brothers" (好兄弟). To make it edible, Buddhists spend many hours reciting sutras, and conduct ceremonies such as the Buddhist Ceremony of Water and Land (水陸法會), *Yu-lan-*

Banners and lanterns at the temple gate guide the "hungry ghosts" to the banquet inside. (Photo by Chen Chih-hsiang)

Water lanterns are released at midnight to invite the spirits of drowned people to join the banquet. (Photo by Chen Chih-hsiang)

Burning lanterns light the way for the "good brothers."
(Photo by Chen Chih-hsiang)

pen (盂蘭盆, from the Sanskrit *avalambana*), or simply *Pu-du* (普渡; universal ferrying). These may be public or private, and take place at any time although the fifteenth (full moon) of the seventh month is most popular.

The *avalambana* is said to derive from the Buddha's disciple Maudgalyayana (木蓮; *mu-lian* in Chinese), who discovered his dead mother in infernal torment, unable to eat any of the food he offered her. The Buddha told him to feed all abandoned souls, firstly preparing the food by prayers.

Food and other offerings are donated by local dignitaries and affluent families who spend large amounts of money to ensure the community's peace at this time. Floating or hanging lanterns are also displayed to guide the returning ghosts. Buddhists and Daoists both celebrate this event, and ceremonies officiated by monastics and priests may last several days. Buddhist temples also construct "*dharma* boats," sometimes made of joss money. These symbolize the "ferrying" (渡) involved in salvation.

Offerings of vast quantities of joss money mean the air is often thick with smoke throughout 8/15. (Photo by Wang Neng-yu)

For Buddhists, this event also marked the end of the traditional 90 days the monastic community spent together over the summer; for Daoists, this is also the "Middle *Yuan*" (中元), a celebration of the birthday for the celestial official responsible for earth (and forgiving sins) Di-guan (地官).

These great festivals also developed into the custom of "grabbing the flag" (搶旗) in which flags are mounted dozens of feet up in the air at the end of a bamboo framework and greasy poles. Capturing the flag is rewarded with rice and money, while the flag may be sold to sailors to ensure safety at sea.

(Near Taipei, these events may be seen in Banqiao and Ilan's Toucheng.)

Operas and ritual dances are performed to entertain the ghosts during their banquet. (Photo by Chen Chih-hsiang)

Mid-Autumn Festival — *The Moon Goddess and the Divine Archer (a Tale of Yin and Yang)*

15th day of the 8th lunar month (8 月 15 日)

With today's practices of moon-gazing (賞月), barbeques and gifts of "moon cakes," it is easy to overlook the religious origins of the Mid-Autumn Festival (中秋節), one of China's "three major festivals."

The full moon of the eighth lunar month is said to be the nearest, largest and most beautiful moon of the year. This event celebrates the moon, and its *yin* connotations of femininity, decay and darkness.

Agricultural Origins

The festival combines aspects of ancient nature worship, in which the moon was a goddess in her own right (太陰星君; Stellar Ruler of Supreme *Yin*) partnering the god of the sun (太陽星君; Stellar Ruler of Supreme *Yang*), as well as the pre-harvest festivities at the end of a spring and summer of agricultural toil. To these, are added elements from later myths, possibly influenced by the arrival of Buddhism from India, the local reaction of formal Daoism, and historical tales regarding the traditional moon-cake fare.

Even by historical times, these religious origins were already blurred. Han dynasty records state that Emperor Wu Di (武帝; 187-140 BCE) initiated three days of partying, which including viewing the moon from the Toad Terrace. The custom survived the break-up of China after the Han collapsed in 220 CE, and reappeared with fresh vigor in Tang and subsequent dynasties.

By this time, a prominent story was that of Chang E (嫦娥), who was originally known as Heng E (恆娥) until the character *heng* (恆), part of the personal name of the Tang emperor Mu-zong (穆宗; r. 821-824), became taboo from utterance by the common people. Recounting her story is still a key part of the day's celebrations.

Larceny, Escape, Exile and Drug Manufacture

The story begins with Hou Yi (后羿), who lived some four thousand years ago during the rule of the legendary emperor Yao (堯; trad. 2357-2255 BCE).

This story may have been imported as he is also known as Yi the Barbarian, and many similar stories exist in other cultures' mythologies, including Taiwan's Aborigines'. Hou Yi appears as protagonist in numerous other myths, saving the "black-haired people" by vanquishing the wind spirit, slaying demons and monstrous animals.

Most famously, he shot down nine new suns that had appeared in the sky and were scorching crops and threatening humankind's existence. For these acts, he was entitled Shen Yi (神羿; Divine Archer) by Emperor Yao, and rewarded with a pill of immortality by Queen Mother of the West. She warned him not to eat it until he had spent a year in spiritual preparation, practicing meditation and fasting.

Yi's wife, the beautiful Chang E, succumbed to temptation however, and while her husband was away, swallowed the pill. Becoming lighter and lighter, she started to float upwards. On Hou Yi's return she was "no larger than a toad" and, as he attempted to follow her flight, he was blown back to earth by a powerful wind.

Chang E continued upwards to the cold, barren landscape of the moon, where the only vegetation was a cassia tree. Coughing up the pill's covering, it was instantly transformed into a rabbit as white as jade. Yu Tu (玉兔), the Jade Rabbit, spends his time grinding cinnamon from the cassia tree to make the drug of immortality.

Chinese say that, especially on this day, one can see these figures as well as that of Wu Gang (吳剛), a miscreant banished to the moon during the Han dynasty for misappropriating the secret of immortality. As a punishment, his Sisyphean task on the moon is to cut down the giant cassia tree, which, each time he removes his ax, restores itself.

Hou Yi, meanwhile, gazes angrily across the heavens at his wife, only being reunited at the full moon of each month.

Chang E rises to the moon (temple bas-relief).

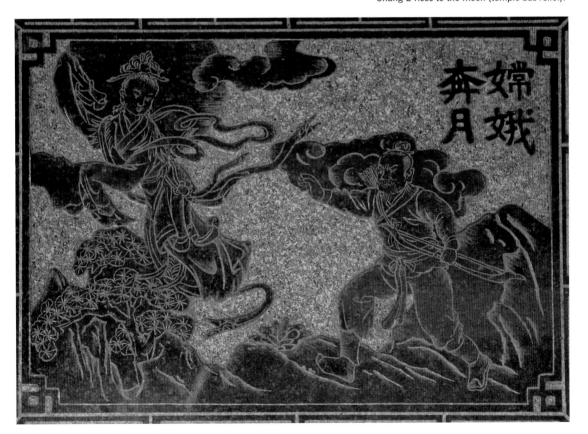

Cosmic concepts

Chang E and Hou Yi's story is really the personification of *yin* and *yang*. In China, like many countries, the moon is feminine and the sun masculine. Furthermore, autumn is the season when *yin* is in the ascendant, the summer's light and heat giving way to darkness and cold, growth ceasing and death imminent.

Temples are packed at Mid-Autumn as worshipers make offerings to various deities.

Cakes, Secret Messages and Rebellion

During the Yuan dynasty, the invading Mongols kept order by billeting one of their own with each tithe-group of ten families, practicing ruthless control. To announce the date of his uprising, rebel leader Zhu Yuanzhang (朱元璋) hit upon the idea of hiding a message inside the moon cakes distributed among Han-Chinese but disdained by the foreign occupiers, who were to be murdered simultaneously throughout the capital at midnight. Evidently, the plan worked, because today, Zhu is better known as Tai Zu (太祖; r 1368-1339), founding emperor of the Ming dynasty.

(Some people may even tell you that Zhu invented moon cakes.)

Pomelos and mooncakes make seasonal offerings.

Of food...

Nowadays, food and wine play an important part in Mid-Autumn celebrations. Moon-round foods are particularly popular, including the grapefruit-like pomelo and moon cakes (月餅). These latter, pastries richly filled with date paste, egg yolks, shredded pork, dried longan and other delicacies, even have their own legend.

...and Poetry

The moon festival was also a timely excuse for spontaneous poetry. Tang dynasty poet and statesman Han Yu (韓愈; 768-824), for example, ends his poem to "Zhang the Clerk,"

Of the year's bright moons, tonight's is the greatest,
human life follows fate, nothing else,
having wine and not drinking it,
what point then the moonlight?

Just as today, the Mid-Autumn Festival was a chance for a get-together with friends and family. In such a large country with officials prohibited from serving in their home province, for many literati this could also be an occasion of sadness at separation from loved ones, as captured by the poet Bai Juyi (白居易; 772-846),

Surely tears fall as we share the bright moon,
a night of homesickness, in five different places.

For China's best-known poet (and wine-lover), Li Bo (李白; 701-762), any moon was an excuse for a poem (and a glass),

I raise my cup to invite the bright moon,
which throws my shadow and we become three.
The moon knows nothing of drinking, however,
and my shadow just follows me around.

According to popular legend, Li Bai died while trying drunkenly to embrace the moon's reflection in a lake.

An Evening of Tranquility

With its moon-gazing, cake-eating and poetry compilation, the Mid-Autumn Festival is certainly more tranquil than most Chinese celebrations when noisy musicians and firecrackers create a "hot and noisy" atmosphere. So perhaps the feminine element really is in the ascendancy. Moreover, as one Chinese idiom advises, "Men must not worship the moon, women must not sacrifice to the Kitchen God."

Master Confucius
— China's "First Teacher"

September 28th (international calendar)

Something of an anomaly as it is celebrated according to the international solar calendar, Confucius' birthday is a great opportunity to participate in a traditional occasion.

Predawn Sacrifice

Like events taking place all around the island on this day, the ceremony at Taipei's Confucius Temple (孔廟; 275 DaTong St.) begins around dawn with three bouts of "drumming solemnity" (鼓嚴) to create a solemn and pious atmosphere for worshiping the sage.

In time to the drum rhythm, the temple "deacons" take up their positions five steps at a time. They are accompanied by invited dignitaries who will participate in the ceremony, and followed by the master of ceremonies and supervisory officials. Finally the chief celebrant (主祭者) takes up his position. All have previous participated in a symbolic hand-washing ceremony and are dressed in temple robes.

Ritual and ceremony have always been central to Confucian teaching.

This is followed by the "Door Opening" (啟扉) of the heavy Ceremonial Doors (儀門) and "Carved-star Doors" (欞星門), which are kept closed at all other times of the year.

Hair and blood from a sacrificed animal (this part is no longer shared with the public) are then "buried" (瘞毛血) in a hole to the west side of the doors.

The sage's spirit is then welcomed (迎神) with more drumming and singing, and four pairs of attendants parading lanterns and swinging censers, followed by six bearers of auspicious implements.

The whole body of celebrants then bows (鞠

Many Taipei schoolyards contain a statue of Confucius, China's first teacher.

Confucius' own descendents are among the dignitaries making offerings at his birthday celebrations.

Lines of dancers move gracefully in the morning light.

Musicians play traditional instruments; one of Confucius' "six arts."

躬) three times.

Offerings of food (進饌) are then made followed by ceremonial presentation of incense (上香) by the main dignitaries usually including the living patriarch of the Kong clan (Confucius is a Latinization of *Kong-fu-zi* 孔夫子; Master Kong) and the Mayor of Taipei, all accompanied by intermittent music, dancing and announcements by the master of ceremonies.

Finally, everyone bows again three times, the doors are closed and the dignitaries troop out again. Afterwards, the atmosphere becomes more relaxed and everyone collects a piece of the sacrificed beast (now made of dough).

Irony

All the pomp that surrounds this worship of the departed spirit of Master Kong is curious given the sage's own injunction,

"To worship an ancestral spirit which is not one's own is obsequious" (非其鬼而祭之，諂也)*

[Tickets are available from the temple office in advance or simply turn up and queue on the day. In any case, well before the 6 a.m. start to ensure a good view.]

---

* [*Analects* II:24]

Double Yang Festival

9th day of the 9th lunar month (9月9日)

Hill walks are believed to be extra-beneficial on Double Ninth Festival.
(Photo by Wang Neng-yu)

In Chinese cosmology, odd numbers are designated to the *yang* principle and even numbers to *yin*. Nine therefore, as three-squared, is the most potent *yang* number, and the 9th day of the 9th lunar month is commonly known as the "Double *Yang* Festival" (重陽節).

Today, although its observance has declined and is usually little more than an excuse for a picnic in the suburbs, certain aspects of its associated customs can be traced back to a story dating from the Eastern Han dynasty (25-220 CE).

Wine, Family and Climbing

Popular legend recounts that a Daoist priest called Fei Chang-fang (費長房), while telling the fortune of a certain Huan Jing (桓景), warned him that on the 9th day of the 9th month he and his family would be in great danger. He suggested that Huan tie a bag of dogwood to his arm and, taking his family with him, climb to a high place where he should drink chrysanthemum wine. Returning home after following this advice, Huan discovered that his pets, fowl and livestock had all suffered violent deaths.

Whether history or legend, this story contains all the key elements of the Double *Yang* Festival's traditional practice over the next two millennia. Friends came together and traveled to the suburbs where they climbed a hill, drunk chrysanthemum wine, roasted meat, and composed and recited poetry. Traditional foods include pickled crabs, persimmons and fish, all served on chrysanthemum petals.

Composed of fermented flowers, chrysanthemum wine is China's best-known medicinal liquor, accredited with curing headaches, paralysis and numerous minor ailments. Dogwood, a bitter herb, is said to ward off evil and was sewn into small pouches, which were fixed to people's clothing.

Traditional cosmological explanations for the effectiveness of Double Ninth customs are that chrysanthemum and dogwood combat the dangers that arise from an excess of *yang*. Perhaps fresh air and exercise were as healthy then as they are today.

The "Blue-eyed Barbarian" —Founder of China's Chan School of Buddhism

5th day of the 10th lunar month (10 月 5 日)

China first learnt of Buddhism during the Han dynasties via contact with traders from the west. This was followed by missionary activities, sometimes encouraged by the state, at other times obstructed. Nevertheless, without sustained contact over succeeding centuries, it is likely that the early ideas of Buddhism, poorly translated and understood even less, would have become merely a sect of Daoism.

One of these later missionaries, Bodhidharma (菩提達摩), who arrived in southern China around 520 CE and died on the banks of the Lu River (魯河) in 534, sowed the initial seeds of what would become the indigenous Chinese school of Chan Buddhism (禪; known in English by the Japanese pronunciation *Zen*). Followers of this sect commemorate his death on the fifth day of the tenth month.

The Blue-eyed Barbarian's ideas were not immediately welcomed, however. Indeed, it is speculated that the disappearance of his first disciple and successor, Hui Ke (慧可), was due to execution. Not a lucky man, Hui was initially rejected by Bodhidharma as not sufficiently steadfast, so had chopped off his own arm to demonstrate his commitment.

One of Bodhidharma's teachings was that realization of one's own buddha-nature is attained through mystic and intuitive practices rather than scriptures and ritual. Having failed to interest the Chinese Buddhist hierarchy in his ideas, he spent nine years in "wall-gazing" meditation, from which he is also known as the "wall-gazing Buddha" (壁觀佛).

Chan Buddhists trace his esoteric teachings back to the historical Buddha himself, who is said to have answered a question from his disciple Kasyapa merely by plucking a flower. Nevertheless, by the tenth century, followers had become too numerous for personal instruction so sutra learning gained a more central role.

Bodhidharma 's elevation to bodhisattva (a being who gives up their own buddhahood to help others) and First Patriarch of the Chan school was due largely to subsequent religious and political developments in China. Elements of his story merged with those of two other important monks, thereby connecting him with the Shaolin Monastery (now famous for its martial art monks).

Routine hagiographical "facts" were also added to this syncretism, making him 150 years old at death, and depicting him as returning to India after death. Hearing this, disciples are said to have opened his grave and found just one straw sandal. Artistic portrayals show Bodhidharma heading for India wearing this one sandal, or legless, having lost the use of his legs during nine years of seated meditation.

Partying with the King of "Green Mountain"

22nd day of the 10th lunar month (10月22日)

Sun Quan (孫權), ruler of the southwestern state of Wu (吳) during the Epoch of the Three Kingdoms (220-265 CE), sent his general, Zhang Gun (張滾), to defend Hui'an (惠安) in Quanzhou Prefecture of Fujian Province. Because "he was wise, brave and upright" and executed his duties with benevolence, he gained the respect of both his fellow soldiers and of the common people.

After his death, local people worshiped him as though he were one of their own ancestors, and all newly arriving officials honored him in their formal ceremonies. A shrine was built in Hui'an, dedicated to him as Wu-de Shen (武德神; Spirit of Soldierly Virtues), and he was accredited with protecting the local area against epidemics. As his fame grew, a cult formed around his name and people of all walks of life prayed to him for peace and prosperity.

In the 10th century, the Song dynasty emperor sent an official named Cui (崔) to govern Hui'an.

As Cui made obeisance to Zhang, the tombstone suddenly collapsed and an inscription of ancient verse was discovered on its back predicting that the emperor would send someone named Cui to take Zhang up Qingshan (青山; Green Mountain). A temple was built on the mountain, and Zhang was enfeoffed as the King of Qingshan (青山王).

Apparently, flags bearing Zhang's name were sufficient to cause the invading Jin army to retreat and in gratitude, the Song emperor Gao Zong (高宗; 1127-1162) promoted Zhang to Honored King of Spiritual Peace (靈安尊王), although to the present day most people call him the King of Green Mountain.

The King of Qingshan's birthday parade is broadcast islandwide on TV.

Colorful characters populate the King's parade.

Overseas Travel

In 1854, wishing to continue to receive his protection, Fujian fishermen brought a statue of Zhang with them to Taiwan. Passing through Bangka (艋舺, today's Wanhua), "the statue became impossibly heavy." Upon inquiry, the god expressed the wish to remain at that location, today's GuiYang Street (貴陽街).

The three-story temple thereafter built there dates from 1856 and has numerous altars and dozens of statues. These include Lao-zi (legendary author of the *Dao-de Jing;* 道德經); the Jade Emperor (玉皇大帝) the supreme deity of Daoism; Guan Yu (關羽), ironically an opposing general during the Epoch of the Three Kingdoms; Mazu (媽祖) the fishermen's goddess; and Sun Wukong (孫悟空), the monkey that accompanied Tripitaka to India in the Buddhist novel *Journey to the West.*

Party of the Year

Each year on the 21st day of the 10th lunar month, the evening before the King's birthday, Zhang's statue is carried around the neighborhood. The next day, the whole district explodes in a riot of noise and color as aged deities are carried on sedan chairs to wish their colleague a happy birthday.

Deities faces are painted with the expressiveness of operatic characters.

"Thinking of the Buddha" Amitabha and the Pureland School

17th day of the 11th lunar month (11月17日)

Perhaps the most common graffito seen around Taipei's streets is 南無阿彌陀佛 (*Na-mo Amituo-Fo*). Scrawled on walls, lampposts and car bumper stickers, it means "Adoration of the Amita Buddha." People even say it when answering the telephone.

It is meant as a constant reminder from believers in the Pureland School of Buddhism (淨土派) that one should think of, or better still, recite the name of a Buddha as often as possible, most often, the Amita Buddha.

The origins of the Amita (Immeasurable Light) Buddha, unknown in Theravada Buddhism, may derive from a monk called Dharmakara who vowed to decline his own buddhahood in order to save others, though some scholars suggest an older origin in India's northwest where Buddhism absorbed Iranian influences.

It was only in 4th-century China, however, that a devotional cult emerged around the recitation of his name, possibly under influence of the Daoist concept of a paradise ruled over by the Queen Mother of the West (西王母).

The popularity of repeated invocation of a deity's name and visualization of supernatural beings grew after persecution of Buddhism in China between 574-578. There was widespread pessimism that in this world of sinners and tyrannical governments, individual effort to achieve enlightenment was futile. Instead, humankind needed a simple path to salvation, aided by the power of Buddha's compassion. If done often enough or at the moment of death, this was said to ensure a person's rebirth in the Pure Land in the West, and subsequently in Nirvana.

Offerings to the Amitha Buddha are often made at the site of traffic accidents.

Chan-Pureland Syncretism

The cult even penetrated Chan monasteries. Superficially, this dependence on an outside agency seems the very opposite of the Chan school's search for one's own buddha-nature. Nevertheless, as D.T. Suzuki has pointed out, in practice, "thinking of the Buddha" is not so different from "holding a koan," in which a Chan aspirant gains inner unity and illumination by reflecting on problems set by a Zen Master.

By late imperial times, a Chan-Pureland syncretized Buddhism was almost universal in China (though not in Japan and Korea). The Chan idea of inner enlightenment was combined with the cult of Amitabha. This resulted in the idea that the true Pureland lies within oneself and that invocation of a holy name can be one theme in Chan meditation.

Amitabha is often depicted as the central figure in a trinity, flanked by Guanyin (觀音; symbolizing compassion), and Da Shizhi (大識智; embodying wisdom).

The Amita Buddha's "birthday" is celebrated on the 17th day of the 11th lunar month.

Celestial Get-together
—And the Bribing of the Kitchen God

24th day of the 12th lunar month (12月24日)

In advance of New Year's arrival, those deities dwelling in the earthly realm and therefore having regular contact with humankind make a trip to heaven to report to the Jade Emperor (玉皇大帝). As they depart on the 24th day of the final month (臘月), people hold a special ceremony, with a corresponding one on the sixth day of the first month when they return.

Lord of the Year

One of the departing deities will not be seen again for another sixty years. This is the Lord of the Year (太歲) of whom there are five dozen, each responsible for one year in the cycle of sixty created by combining one of the ten Heavenly Stems (天干) and twelve Earthly Branches (地支), the ancient means of marking hours and days, though not originally, it seems, years. Statues of all sixty, with a sign announcing the next year in which they will appear, can be seen at the Ci-You Temple (慈祐宮) on BaDe Rd. opposite Songshan Railway Station.

God of the Stove

More popular is the story surrounding Zao Shen (灶神; God of the Stove), made famous in the West by Amy Tan's novel *The Kitchen God's Wife*. Living in the kitchen, where he is often represented by a picture or small statue, he is privy to the household's secrets. Worried about what he might have overheard, on the evening of the 23rd, people smear his mouth with honey, or make offerings to him of sesame, peanut or other sticky candy, to ensure that on arriving in heaven, his "mouth is sweet" or even that his "lips are stuck together" and he cannot speak at all.

No one seems to remember the origins of this custom. One suggestion is that it dates from instructions on "Sacrificial Methods" in the Zhou dynasty (11th-3rd cent. BCE) *Book of Rites* (禮記), which mentions seven sacrifices the king should make on behalf of the clans, one of which was to the hearth. The common people could only make one such sacrifice, possibly to the doorway or perhaps to the hearth. Another explanation is that it may derive from ancient practices involving the worship of fire.

The Kitchen God later acquired a name, Su Ji-li (蘇吉利), while his wife was called Bao Jie (寶姐); while yet another version states that he was originally a beautiful but talkative goddess, who only later become male.

Lord of the year (辛巳年; *Xīn-sì*) waits to make his next appearance in 2061.

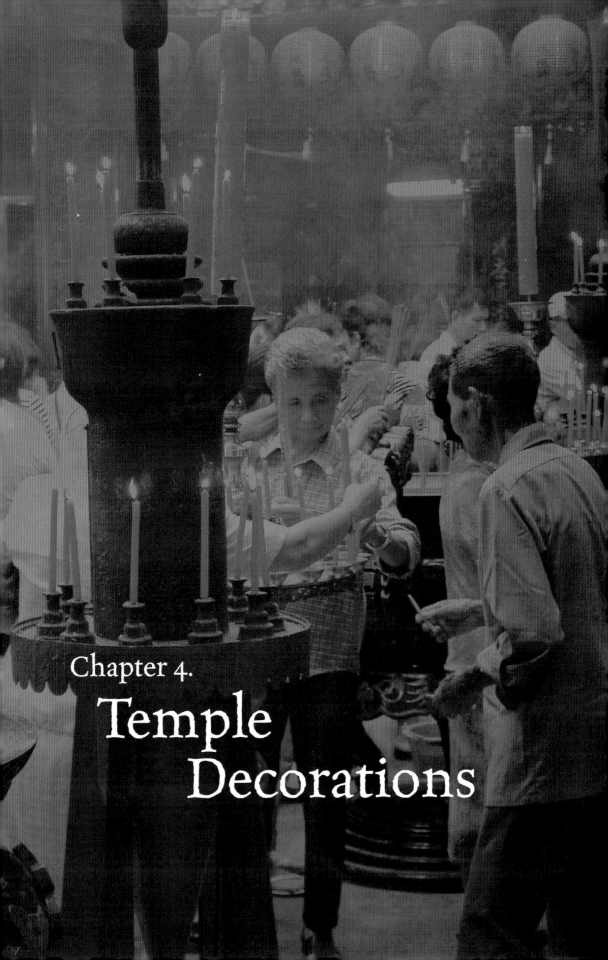

Chapter 4.
Temple Decorations

Doors

Temple doors, bright red with bearded warriors or brass buttons, are not just impressive, they are full of meaning.

Door Gods (門神)

Door gods, auspicious couplets and lions all protect this temple entrance.

Most commonly, a central pair of temple doors is decorated with the images of two gentlemen. These may be either "martial" or "civil" door gods.

a) Shen Shu (神荼) and Yu Lei (鬱壘) lived on Mount Du-shuo (度朔) in the Eastern Sea, where there grew a great peach-tree whose branches covered an area of several thousand square li. The lowest branches formed a Door of Ghosts. Shen Shu and Yu Lei guarded this doorway, binding those who had done harm in reeds and feeding them to tigers.

Recognizing their power over evil, people hung peach-wood tablets (now paper drawings) of their images on their doors to ward off evil.

b) These were later supplanted in people's favor by two ministers of the Tang emperor Tai-zong (太宗; r. 628-649). The emperor had fallen ill and heard demons in his bedchamber. Informed by the imperial physician that their ruler was delirious and in great danger, Qin Shu-bao (秦叔寶) and Yu-chi Jing-de (尉遲敬德) volunteered to keep watch at his door. The next day, the emperor thanked them for his peaceful night's sleep. This continued for some time until the illness diminished, after which the two ministers were allowed to take up their normal duties. Just to be sure, the emperor is said to have had their images painted on his doors to fool any demons still wishing him harm.

Door gods are usually painted in great detail. Even the red background color is thought to be efficacious.

Temple doorways are full of symbols and are by no means simple entrances.

Guardian Kings

Other panels are painted with a variety of figures. For example, originating in Buddhist temples but now found in all kinds of temples, either painted on their doors or as statues inside, are the four *deva* kings (四大天王).

These are Mo-li Qing (魔禮青), armed with a sword, who guards the east. When brandished, his sword produces tens of thousands of spears and a fire that attacks enemies with fiery serpents. Mo-li Hai (魔禮海), armed with a guitar that commands the world's attention, guards the west. Mo-li Hong (魔禮紅), armed with the "umbrella of chaos," which is capable of plunging the world into darkness and producing violent thunderstorms and earthquakes, guards the south. Finally, Mo-li Shou (魔禮壽), armed with a man-eating snake, guards the north.

Mo-li Qing is armed with a magical sword.

Guardian Lions

Following the influence of Buddhist temples, many secular buildings and even some graves have a pair of white carved lions on guard outside. That their curly knotted hair, round faces and fang-like teeth are only vaguely recognizable as lionesque is because the few animals imported to China were for the emperor's entertainment and would never have been seen by temple craftsmen, who merely heard their ferocious nature described at tenth-hand.

Mo-li Hai's guitar commands the world's attention.

Stone lions guard buildings of any importance.

The left lion is female, usually playing with a cub; the right is male and paws an ornamental ball. Originally, the number of bumps on their head indicated the rank of the official whose building they guarded.

Occasionally, the pair will be Korean Dogs, of which one is a lion, the other a dog. These can be distinguished by their mouths: the lion is roaring (mouth open); the dog is growling (mouth closed).

Most temple entrances have thresholds, which should be stepped over carefully.

Main Doors and Threshold

Visitors to many temples should use the side doors not the main, central doors which are reserved for use by deities. Similarly, the thresholds (門檻) of all doorways should be stepped over, never on. Originally meant to prevent vehicles from entering, thresholds are now said to be places at which ghosts congregate.

Algal Wells

The ceilings just inside each door are ornately decorated and painted. These are known as algal wells (藻井) and, in addition to their aesthetic function, are present to trick evil spirits into thinking the temple is underwater and cannot, therefore, be burnt down. Not surprisingly, with so many candles and incense around, this was a common fate for temples in bygone times.

Many temple beams are decorated with dragons with fish bodies for the same reason.

An "algal well" embedded in the temple ceiling just inside the entrance to warn malevolently inclined spirits not to waste their time.

The Lotus
— *Pure Flower-Pure Mind*

Lotuses are among the most common decorative themes in temples throughout the city. In addition to their beautifying function, their symbolism is to remind temple-goers of the purity of spirituality.

Growing in ponds, the lotus rises out of the mud but is itself unsullied. It is inwardly empty, outwardly upright, has no branches and smells sweetly. For a long time it has symbolized the purity of Buddhism.

Buddhas and bodhisattvas are frequently depicted on lotus thrones (蓮座), the lotus position is adopted for meditation (蓮坐), the "Lotus Nation" (蓮邦) is an alternative name for the Pureland of the Amitha Buddha, monks' and nuns' robes are nicknamed "lotus garments" (蓮花衣), the Lotus Sect (蓮宗) was founded in China in the 4th century CE, and the White Lotus Society (白蓮社) was a quasi-religious secret society during the Yuan dynasty. The fruit, flower and stalk of the lotus symbolize the past, present and future Buddhas.

The lotus pond in Taipei's Botanical Gardens is popular for religious contemplation and secular art.

The *Lotus Sutra* (妙法蓮華經) is one of Mahayana Buddhism's key texts, called by its 1930 translator W.E. Soothill, "the most important religious book of the Far East." Its Mahayana supporters claim it is the final and consummate teaching of the Śākyamuni historical Buddha; followers of the older Theravada school are equally vehement that it is not.

The *Lotus Sutra* is a manifesto of Mahayana doctrine, portraying the Buddha in terms of religious adulation and romanticized myth. It also contains the oldest references to the Bodhisattva Avalokiteśvara, "Regarder of the World's Cries" (Guanyin 觀音 in Chinese), who is often portrayed as the "lotus-holding bodhisattva" (持蓮觀音).

In Daoism, the lotus is a symbol of He Xian-gu (何仙姑), one of the Eight Immortals, possibly because of the similarity between her surname, He (何), and another word for lotus (荷; he).

Various other words punning with either蓮 (*lian*) or 荷 (*he*) mean that lotuses are often used in "word-play" art, popular with Chinese. Wedding gifts, for example, often portray lotus flowers to imply "love" (戀; *lian*), "to join together" (連; *lian*), "unison" (合; *he*) and "peace" (和; *he*).

With so much religious and artistic symbolism, the lotus has a secure position in the Chinese heart and subconscious. Their blossoming in early summer is greeted by flocks of visitors who photograph, paint or merely enjoy this favorite flower.

Buddhist monastics meditate in the "lotus position."

Buddhist art showing *mudra* (hand gesture) and lotus flower.

The Lotus Effect

Interestingly, over the last two or three decades, scientists are proving what Buddhists and Hindus have said for millennia, that lotuses are clean, operating a kind of self-cleaning process. In particular, the great sacred lotus (*Nelumbo nucifera*) removes water from its surface through a combination of chemical repulsion and a corrugated surface. Water droplets run off, taking dirt with them. This has led to development of products like Lotusan, a silicon coating for houses, and Lotus Effect roof tiles and self-cleaning glass.

The Eight Auspicious Objects

Although the lotus might be the most widespread Buddhist symbol, it is only one of eight Auspicious Objects used to characterize various aspects of Buddhism, and which appear as a group, sometimes even displayed on temple altars.

These are:

1. The conch, which symbolizes the *dharma* (法) natural laws and teachings of the Buddha. Appropriate to each person's personality, it awakens them from the "slumber of ignorance" to fulfill their buddha-nature.

2. Just as an umbrella protects its user from the sun or rain, Buddhism protects people from harmful forces and obstacles that would otherwise perpetuate life's suffering and prevent awakening and enlightenment. The umbrella's shade is also likened to the *sangha* (僧; Buddhist community).

3. The victory banner symbolizes the victory of body, speech and mind over obstacles and negative forces.

4. The lotus symbolizes the complete purification of bodily defilements, speech and mind, and the full blossoming of blissful liberation.

5. The vase, although symbolizing wealth, actually teaches the value of inner preciousness of moral discipline and the study and practice of *dharma* for the benefit of oneself and others. As vessels for flowers, vases symbolize seasonal change and impermanence.

6. The double fish emblem teaches followers not to fear drowning in the "sea of suffering" (苦海) but to move spontaneously from place to place, in harmony with one's own self and others.

7. The endless knot (盤長) symbolizes the mutual dependence of religious teachings and secular affairs; the union of wisdom and expedient method; the inseparability of emptiness and "dependent arising;" and finally, at enlightenment, the union of wisdom and compassion.

8. The *dharma* wheel (法輪) is both the "wheel of law" that rolls forward without pause, crushing evil in its path and spreading wisdom, and the "wheel of Buddha's teaching," the turning of which represents the passing of these teachings from master to disciple, from one generation to the next, enabling all beings to discover their buddha-nature and to experience liberation.

Perhaps influenced by the above, Daoism has a similar array of eight objects, associated with the Eight Immortals (八仙), which are also found in temple decorations. These are the fan, sword, bottle-gourd, castanets, flower basket, bamboo cane, flute, and lotus.

There are various other groups of eight items, such as the eight treasures of Confucianism, though this group may be reduced to four or expanded to fourteen.

These eight items are (wishing) pearls, musical stone, coin, rhombus, books, paintings, rhinoceros horn and Artemisia leaf (yarrow).

Dragons
— The Good, the Bad
and the Composite Beast

The proliferation of dragon images at both secular buildings and temples shows the benign, even sacred, nature of the Chinese dragon in comparison with the fire-breathing, damsel-snatching monsters of Occidental mythology. The latter, probably developed from serpents (despised in the Christian Bible and elsewhere), so that slaying a dragon in the Occident is tantamount to killing the snake that tempted Eve and led to humankind being cast out from the Garden of Eden.

Mythological or Biological Origins

First appearing at least 8,000 years ago, the Chinese dragon is also of great antiquity and, perhaps, even more obscure origin. Four main theories exist. These are that

1. Dragons really exist or did so during a certain period of human history.

2. They are derived from another animal which does, or once did, exist.

3. They represent a combination of various animals.

4. They are derived from non-biological sources.

Dragon motif in lacquer on temple door.

Real Dragons

Dragons are so well established in Chinese mythology, literature and psyche that, until recently, people took their real existence for granted. In a culture that accepts the reality of gods, ghosts and spirits mingling with humankind in the earthly realm, belief in non-visible creatures with magical powers is relatively straightforward.

If more evidence was needed, mention of dragons in the inscriptions of "oracle bones," China's oldest systematic script, was taken as evidence that, in great antiquity, humans and dragons walked the earth together. (Oracle bones were previously known as "dragon bones" and ground up for use in traditional medicines.)

Strange Animals

Various animals have been put forward as possible inspiration for ancient people's tales of dragons.

The earliest known versions of 龍 (*long*), the written character for dragon strongly resembled the word for snake with an altered head. Perhaps, therefore, a cobra or other species of snake underlies the word's etymology. Promotion of snake to dragon would be natural for ancestral people who worshiped the snake totem.

Other suggestions include crocodiles, sea horses and ammonites (early depictions of dragons were often executed in jade or other semi-precious stones), or the fossil remains of some species of dinosaur. Early depictions of short-legged, crawling dragons indicate some kind of giant lizard. Other archaeological and ethnological evidence supports a large, migratory fish which, swimming up rivers

Unusually ferocious dragon in bas-relief (temple decoration).

in the spring, gave rise to the superstition that the coming of dragons marked the time for sowing crops. Dragons are still believed to live in seas and rivers, and to ascend to the clouds and cause rain. As such they were, and still are, symbols of fertility.

Animal Totems

The Han-Chinese race of today resulted from the coalescence of various Neolithic peoples, each with its own culture, mythology and religious practices. One aspect of this was the worship of different animal totems, often related to creation or virgin birth legends. An ancestor of the Shang dynasty royal family, for example, became pregnant after eating a blackbird's egg; and the Zhou progenitor gave birth after treading in a bear's footprint.

Dragons were possibly another such totem or, more likely, a composite animal created by the gradual unification of these various peoples. They have long been portrayed as having deer antlers, snake bodies, fish scales, eagle claws, camel head, ox ears, cockle abdomen, a wispy goat beard and so forth. (Interestingly, the mythologies of China's ethnic minorities who were left out of this ancient federation often portray dragons as an evil threat.)

Dragon and "auspicious clouds" (temple decoration).

Dragon (*yang*) and *feng* (*yin*) as decorations
on temple joss-money incinerator roof.

Physical Phenomena

One final theory is that dragons derive from physical phenomena such as cyclones (dragon rotating winds; 龍旋風), or strange shapes imagined during lightning storms and accompanied by the "roar" of thunder. This latter fits with the explanation that dragons hibernate in deep water through the winter before reappearing in spring, the common season for lightning storms in China.

Imperial Usurpation

In a "modern" twist of the virgin birth myth, the mother of Liu Bang (劉邦; r.206-194 BCE), first emperor of the Han dynasty, is said to have dreamt she met a god, felt the dragon's presence, and became pregnant. For the two thousand years of China's imperial history, dragons were a personal emblem of the emperor and, from the Ming dynasty onwards, unofficial depiction became illegal.

Today dragons also represent the *yang,* male force and, as such, are paired with a *yin* phoenix-like *feng* (鳳).

Crouching Tigers

Second only to dragons as temple decorations are tigers.

After making offerings and prayers to the temple's main deity and other subsidiary ones of their choice, temple visitors will often light a few sticks of incense as an offering and place them before the sculpture of a tiger found crouching beneath the altar or in a wall niche nearby. More elaborate offerings might include a slice of "five-color meat" (五花彩肉), a duck egg or piece of yellow tofu.

Obscure Pedigree

This is no ordinary tiger but Lord Tiger (虎爺), about whose origins there are various myths. One such connects him with "The Great Emperor Who Pre-serves Life" (保生大帝), patron deity of Taipei's Bao-an Temple (保安宮), who is said to have once helped heal a tiger. In gratitude, tigers took up guard outside his temple, later being promoted to the deity Lord Tiger.

Another legend links him to Fu-de Zheng-jun (福德正君), otherwise known as Lord of the Land. Seemingly, tigers were bullying all the less ferocious animals

Most tigers are in fact Lord Tiger, worshiped in his own right.

of the forest which, therefore, beseeched the Lord's help. He appointed the tiger as his messenger and, because Lord of the Land is a key deity responsible for good harvests and financial success, people began to make offerings and pray to Lord Tiger as well.

Another explanation is that he perhaps derives from Chinese nature worship practices or from an ancient totem. Tiger designs have been found on pottery dated to the Chinese Neolithic period and appear widely during the subsequent Shang and Zhou dynasties. There was also overlap with legendary animals, such as the depiction of *taotie* (饕餮; a ferocious and gluttonous beast) faces on tiger bodies.

Tigers are primarily revered for their ferocity. Able to bite demons and evil spirits, they make good protectors of temples and, by extension, against certain diseases that were diagnosed as being caused by malevolent spirits. Cure of the children's illness mumps, for example, which in Chinese is nicknamed "pig-head plague" (豬頭瘟) because the head and mouthparts swell, was entrusted to appeal to Lord Tiger because "tiger bites pig."

Lord Tiger often appears below the foot of Fu-de Zheng-jun, for whom he works.

"Dipper" Lanterns
—Barrels of Family Protection

Dipper lanterns contain an assortment of symbolic instruments.

Small barrels filled with rice, into which are inserted a "treasured sword" (寶劍), scissors, steelyard, ruler, mirror, lamp-oil bowl, parasol and images of the Southern and Northern Constellations, are a ubiquitous feature of temple worship in Taipei. Sometimes single and magnificently ornate, during Daoist *jiao* ceremonies (醮祭), these "Dipper" Lanterns (斗燈) may be fashioned from paper and card by the hundreds and fill every spare inch of the temple. They require some explanation, however.

The name *Dou Deng* (斗燈) is a play on words as 斗 both means a rice measure and occurs in the names of two Stellar Sovereigns, the Southern Dipper (南斗) and Northern Dipper (北斗). "Dipper" lanterns thus include a barrel of rice and images of the seven stars of the Northern Dipper.

Assorted Objects

The square-shaped barrel symbolizes earth; the circular parasol represents the heavens. Rice is the most important of the Five Grains of antiquity and symbolizes the continuity of life. The sword and scissors are weapons to exorcise bad luck, the steelyard measures a family's allotment of fortune, the ruler is used to judge right and wrong.

On the left, a Seven-star Sword made of peach-wood represents the Green Dragon (青龍; guarding the east) and symbolizes the dispelling of evil. On the right, the steelyard represents the White Tiger (白虎; west) and symbolizes law. At the front, the scissors represent the Vermillion Finch (朱雀; south) and symbolize the extermination of evil monsters. At the back, the ruler represents Xuan-Wu (玄武; a combination of Black Turtle and Snake, guardian of the north) and symbolizes awesome spiritual power. The circular mirror placed in the center symbolizes the brightness of the primal star.

Other objects symbolize longevity (associated with the Southern Constellation), courage, anger, wealth, many descendents and so forth. The Five Elements underlying Chinese cosmology are represented in the clay pot (土; earth), wick holder (金; metal), cotton wick (木; wood), water (水) mixed with oil, and fire (火) when the lantern is lit.

These lanterns are used during *jiao* ceremonies to pray for a family's good fortune. The candle is lit and offerings are made to the Stellar sovereigns. Stars or sacred sayings are drawn on strips of paper and hung beneath the parasol.

Small dipper lanterns used in Daoist temple ceremonies are then taken home for security and family prosperity.

Offerings of Fruit

Offerings placed on temple and home altars are gifts for deities and ancestral spirits (and cannot be touched by the living until the unseen have eaten their fill, which may be ascertained using divinatory blocks). Many also have symbolic meaning, especially fruit, often through the Chinese passion for word play.

Apples and Pears

Apples (蘋果; *ping-guo*), for example, are suggestive of "peace" (平; *ping*).

Oranges (橘; *ju*), sound like "to wish" (祝; *zhu*) in Mandarin; or "auspicious" (吉; *ji*) in Taiwanese (indeed, the character is often written as 桔).

Persimmons (柿; *shi*) sound like "affairs" (事), so oranges and persimmons together suggest "may you have good fortune in all your undertakings."

Pomegranates' many seeds (子) also represent the good fortune of "many sons and many grandsons" (多子多孫).

Jujubes (棗; *zao*) sound like "early" (早; *zao*), so are paired with lichees (which have a large seed) at weddings to mean "may you soon have many sons, " or with cinnamon (桂; *gui*) to symbolize "may you soon attain nobility (貴; *gui*)."

Peaches represent longevity and peach-wood is said to repel demons and evil spirits.

Pears (梨; *li*) are also a symbol of longevity

Examination time offerings of celery (芹; *qin*) symbolizing "diligence" (勤勞; *qin-lao*) and turnips (Taiwanese: 菜頭; *tsai-tao*) symbolizing "good sign" (好彩頭; *ho tsai-tao*).

because pear trees can live a long time. They will rarely be found on altars however, because of the homophonic word "separation" (離).

Longan, which literally means "dragon eyes" (龍眼), are therefore associated with the power and majesty of that creature.

Finger lemons, which fill the temple with their sweet smell, are called "Buddha's hand" (佛手; *fo-shou*) as long, thin fingers are said to be one of the thirty-two distinguishing signs of a buddha. Furthermore, because of a similar pronunciation, this fruit also symbolizes a "happy and long life" (福壽; *fu shou*).

Apricots are a metaphor for the teaching profession because Confucius is said to have taught in the "apricot arena" (杏壇).

Pineapples (鳳梨; *feng-li*) are often given the pride of place on temple altars because the Taiwanese pronunciation *ong-lai* puns with "prosperity has come" (旺來), though not in Mandarin.

The Ru-Yi
— *"As One Wishes"*

Many deities and other temple figures may be seen holding a small curved scepter, known as a *ru-yi* (如意), meaning "as one wishes."

Origins of this "wish-fulfilling scepter" are long forgotten; some people say they are the spiritual equivalent of tablets held by officials when in audience with an emperor, others that they are the insignia of celestial emperors. In secular use, they symbolize a scholar or official, and are given at a wedding by the groom's family to that of the bride in the hope that the marriage will go "as one wishes."

Buddhist scholars suggest it derives from a short sword or from the lotus. Some anthropologists think it may be the symbol of an ancient phallic cult.

Yet another theory, supported by the design of many *ru-yi* in the shape of a large-headed fungus, links them to ancient magical practices involving a dark-colored fungus *Ganoderma lucidum* (靈芝) supposed to possess supernatural powers. If so, they may be a symbol of ancient people's search for immortality, or in the use of natural hallucinogens for spiritual enlightenment.

Temple deity holding *ru-yi* scepter.

Chapter 5.

Written Documents

Reciting Sutras

Chinese "folk" religion, with which this book is primarily concerned, does not have a central text like the *Qu'ran* or *Bible.* Even the Three Religions, which constitute the building blocks (sometimes concrete; at other times shadowy) of this popular religious practice, have large collections of texts, such as the *Thirteen Classics* (十三經) of Han dynasty Confucianism; the "Treasury" (藏) of Buddhism, which is commonly called the *Tripitaka* (三藏) of *sutras* (經), *vinaya* (律) and *sastras* (論); and the "*Daoist Treasury*" (道藏) composed of thousands of volumes.

Lay practitioners recite scriptures around the clock at the Xing Tian Temple.

A temple visit may bring one into contact with various texts. In addition to the *Book of Changes* (易經) and other written tools of divination, most commonly, perhaps, will be scriptures heard recited by monastic or lay groups kneeling before the altar.

The language is arcane and archaic, so that even uninitiated Taipei citizens will not understand much. Moreover, not only are special texts read in accordance with special events, but each temple has its own favored texts.

Daoist Canon

Xing Tian Temple, for example, generally uses ten texts; many, such as the *Classic of the Sage Emperor Guan* (關聖帝君的經典), relate to Guan-di, the main deity among five worshiped there. Most of these are found in the official Daoist canon; one such, the *Classic of Supreme Gentleman Lao Explains Tranquility* (太上老君說清靜經), refers to Lao-zi (老子) and through him to *The Classic of Virtue and its Way* (道德經), said to have been written by him.

One of the major texts of the school of "philosophic" Daoism, its opening is well known and often quoted:

The Way that can be spoken
　　is not the constant Way. (道可道非常道)
The name that can be named
　　is not the constant name. (名可名非常名)

It continues by explaining that that which has no name is the origin of heaven and earth, and the mother of all things. This basic cosmology is detailed as the Way producing the One; the One giving rise to the Two (*yin* and *yang*); the Two giving rise to the Three (Heaven, Earth and Man); and the Three giving rise to the myriad things.

Daoism subsequently placed great emphasis on trying to harmonize oneself (as well as one's community and state) with these elemental forces, and such themes underlie many of the scriptures recited at Daoist temples as well as those dedicated to deities outside the official Daoist pantheon.

The Universal Door Sutra is read every evening at Taipei's Longshan Temple.

Buddhist Canon

Recitation of scriptures is also a common feature at Buddhist temples and monasteries, especially at "morning class" (早課) and "evening class" (晚課). The *Heart Sutra* (心經) and *Universal Door Sutra* (普門經) recited at Taipei's Longshan Temple are typical.

The latter has been discussed earlier in context of the development of the bodhisattva Guanyin as a key figure in Mahayana Buddhism. It is the 25th chapter of the *Lotus Sutra* (妙法蓮華經), which introduces the idea that by calling on the assistance of Guanyin (Regarder of [the World's] Cries), one may attain salvation. It is, therefore, a defining change in Buddhism from seeking enlightenment for the few to salvation of the many, a "Universal Door" to Nirvana.

The Heart Sutra, on the other hand, although it is also a Mahayana text and begins with an appeal to the authority of Avalokiteśvara (Guanyin), lays down a more theoretical approach to enlightenment, through *prajna* (*dharma* wisdom) and an understanding of the non-existence of self.

The *Prajna-paramita* Heart Sutra

When the bodhisattva Avalokiteśvara was practicing the deep *prajna-paramita**, He saw that each of the five *skandhas*[+] of human existence was empty, and thus overcame all suffering and adversity.

"OŚariputra[++], form does not differ from the Void; the Void does not differ from form.

Form is the Void; the Void is form. Feeling, Conception, Impulse and Consciousness are also like this; empty.

OŚariputra, thus everything is illusory;

---

* Prajna is the sixth of ten paramita, the means of crossing the Sea of Suffering, that is, attaining liberation on the other shore of Nirvana. The other paramita include charity, moral conduct, patience and abnegation of self.

+ *Skandha,* literally "something which covers," in Buddhism it is used to refer to the physical and mental forms which obstruct the realization of truth. The *sutra* continues to enumerate these. (Chinese: 蘊)

++ Śariputra, a disciple of Buddha

Reciting sutras is a means of creating good merit.

Neither arising nor extinguished; neither impure nor pure; neither increasing nor diminishing.

Therefore, in the Void, there is no form. There is no Feeling, Conception, Impulse or Consciousness.

There is no eye, ear, nose, tongue, body nor mind. There is no form, sound, smell, taste, touch nor *dharma*.

There is no realm of vision. Then reaching the realm of no consciousness;

No ignorance as well as no limit to ignorance;

Reaching no old age and death as well as no limit to old age and death;

There is no suffering, no attachments that cause suffering; nor the extinction of these attachments, nor the way to extinction. There is no wisdom as well as no attainment.

Because there is nothing to be attained, a Bodhisattva availing of *prajna-paramita* has no obstructions in his mind. Because there is no obstruction, there is no fear.

He passes beyond deluded thinking to ultimate Nirvana.

The Buddhas of the past, present and future, availing of *prajna-paramita,* attained supreme, complete enlightenment.

Thus the *prajna-paramita* is the great divine mantra; the great mantra of illumination, the supreme mantra without equal.

It can expel all suffering. Itself is real and not illusory."

He therefore recited the *prajna-paramita* mantra, saying "*Gati, Gati, Boluo Gati. Boluo Seng Gati. Bodhi Svaha**"

While seeking alms, this Buddhist monk counts prayer recitations on his prayer beads.

---

* This is interpreted as: "Go (on the path of accumulating merit), go (on the path of preparation), go perfectly (onto the path of seeing things as they really are), go perfectly beyond (onto the path of habituation), buddhahood, so-be-it!"

Charms, Amulets and Talismans
—Personal Protection at Home and Abroad

Just as mirrors above lintels and stone lions beside doors are *feng-shui* techniques designed to protect a home or other building from evil spirits, so the people of Taipei adorn their bodies with jade bracelets, lockets containing incense ash, or small parcels containing scribbled writing drawn frantically by men possessed by spirits.

Portable *Feng-shui*

Talismans can be made of almost any material and often draw on historic or legendary themes. Some, like jade objects or the characters of a heroic figure's name, can be traced to distinct origins; others, such as the use of peach-wood, are long forgotten and often consigned to "superstition."

Jade *cong* in the National Palace Museum collection.

The Power and Authority of Jade

China passed through a Jade Age at the end of its Stone Age, during which, the increased hardness and luster of jade gave rulers of the Shang and Zhou dynasties both a real and symbolic edge over the common people, just as iron-working and other metallurgical technology conferred advantages on a later generation.

"Authority jade" emblems such as *gui* (珪) were held by nobles while attending court. Similarly, earthly rulers held "worship jades" when petitioning heaven. Circular *bi* (璧) and rectangular *cong* (琮) jades were also used to represent the spherical heavens and square earth and thus act as conduits to bring gods to the human realm.

Jade was also accredited with the supernatural power to ward off ghosts and evil spirits. A jade ornament was said to prevent a rider being thrown from his horse and eating jade was said to relieve people from the limits imposed by gravity.

Jade ornaments were placed in the palms and orifices of the dead to protect them in the netherworld. Han emperors had whole funerary suits made of jade joined with gold wire.

Today, hardly a person in Taipei does not possess at least one jade bracelet or pendant, their aesthetic value often secondary to their use as an amulet. Surprisingly, if such an item is broken, it is said that it is "bad luck that has broken."

"Tiger Soul" and Other Animal Powers

Hu-po (琥珀), the Chinese word for amber, is said to derive from the belief that after a tiger (虎; *hu*) dies, its soul (魄; *po*) enters the ground and is transformed into amber. Amulets made from this fossilized pine resin are therefore credited with imbuing their owners with the courage of this fierce animal.

Others use tiger claws as a charm. Pictures or statues of bears are also believed to guard a home against spiritual dangers and even the more earthly worries of theft.

A lock of an infant's hair may be mixed with dog's hair and sewn inside clothing for protection against the Heavenly Dog (天狗), also known as the Child-stealing Devil (偷生鬼), originally a young girl who died unmarried and is trying to kill a child for whom she can substitute, thereby gaining reincarnation.

Children are often dressed from "head-to-tail" (頭尾) with tiger clothes, or given finely embroidered tiger shoes or a tiger hat (小虎帽). Sometimes, a child will be given the name of an animal to compensate for some perceived character flaw.

Plowshares into Swords

Wearing small pieces of old iron plowshares hung around the neck, sometimes wrapped in cloth or paper, or with a point projecting, illustrates the veneration still felt for Shen Nong, Fu Xi and other mythical figures. The modern explanation is that, "evil spirits are warded off by the sharp point."

Iron nails used in sealing a coffin (after exhumation) are also considered good at warding off evil. Hammered thin, they may be worn as necklaces, bracelets or anklets.

Copper coins are also popular. Joined together with red thread into the shape of a sword, for example, they are hung at the head of a bed to protect sleepers (when their soul might be absent or reduced in strength), in the rooms of sick people, or where someone has committed suicide or suffered a violent death. The protective power comes from the emperor whose reign name appears on the

Written by priests or *ji-tong* at the local temple, almost indecipherable talismans are taken home and used to ward off evil spirits.

Usually used by motorcyclists and car drivers, even this infant in his walker-chair has a talisman for protection.

coins. Strong and successful rulers are preferred, though sometimes auspicious characters in an emperor's name are sufficient. Coins from the Tang and Song dynasties are particularly popular, as well as combinations of the Kang-xi (康熙) and Shun-zhi (順治) reign periods during the Qing dynasty, as together these spell out "healthy, prosperous and smooth regulation."

In a modern variation on this theme, train tickets used to travel between auspicious-sounding railway stations have been incorporated into amulets.

For some reason, five-zhu (銖; $^1/_{24}$th of a tael) coins dating from the Former Han dynasty (206 BCE-25 CE) are greatly prized, and may be found at "antiques" stalls reproduced in jade or precious metals. In fact, nearly all the coins found for sale will be reproductions. For Taipei people, however, these are not fakes, as it is the emperor's name that is talismanic and not the age of the coin.

Sometimes a few coins are hung around the neck of City God or other favored temple statue, then taken home and worn by children. Alternatively, one coin is added to the necklace each year of the child's life until he or she reaches 15, by which time the danger presented by the "thirty barriers" (關) has passed. These barriers go by exotic names such as Barrier of the Broken Bridge (斷橋關), Barrier of the Heavenly Dog (天狗關), Barrier of Deep Water (深水關), and Barrier of Scalding Soup (湯火關).*

Power of the Written Word

For a largely illiterate society in which advancement came through scholarship on ancient texts, the written language represented something to be venerated (indeed, in Chinese mythology, the discovery of writing was divinely inspired). Even today, many people burn any paper that has writing on it rather than disposing of it casually. Formerly, houses were equipped with a box marked "respect and treat with care paper that has script," into which scraps of printed paper were put until they could be burnt reverently.

Particularly efficacious for use in personal protection are said to be passages from religious texts or charms written by priests. These can be seen everywhere, pasted on doors and walls, hanging from motorcycle handlebars and car mirrors, or pinned to a child's clothing. For truly internal *feng-shui,* a "burn ash and swallow talisman" (燒灰吞符) is written on yellow paper, burnt, the ashes mixed with water and the whole thing swallowed. Similarly, the ash of incense offered to a favored deity at a local temple may be diluted and drunk, or placed inside a locket and worn around the neck.

This kind of pendant is often in shape of a lock. Placing it around a child's neck is said to "lock the child to life." One traditional custom is for a parent to solicit a small amount of money from one hundred family members and friends. This is used to buy a "hundred families lock" (百家鎖), which has the surety of one hundred people in addition to spiritual protection. (Poorer communities use "hundred family tassels" (百家線) to which friends are asked to contribute a colored thread.)

Locks may also be made from peach-wood or peach-kernels, as the peach symbolizes longevity and its wood is said to ward off evil spirits. Spring couplets pasted around doorframes at Chinese New Year originated as boards of peach-wood, to which powerful written slogans were added later.

Further protection can be given a child by engraving a small metal plate with the Eight Terms (八

---

* The full list is given in *Outlines of Chinese Symbolism and Art Motives* by C.A.S. Williams, 1941; p.73.

字) of his or her horoscope, or the corresponding animal sign of the zodiac. This too, may be hung on a necklace or attached to clothing.

Spiritual power to defeat malevolent spirits

Two of the most popular forms of talisman in today's Taipei are those written in Tibetan (often the bodhisattva Avalokitesvara's mantra, "*om mani peme hung*"), and those written by *ji-tong* (乩童; divinatory boys).

Possessed by a deity or other spirit, the *ji-tong* beat themselves with torture implements until they draw blood (said to be that of the deity not their own and, therefore, of great potency), which is used along with regular ink by the possessed person to write talismans. These are generally indecipherable to the uninitiated but treasured dearly. Stamped with the deities' seal and kept next to their statues on the temple altar, the "sealed spells" (印符) are taken home by the gathered adherents for use in *feng-shui,* personal protection, or as gifts to sick or endangered relatives.

Talismans can be attached anywhere for portable protection.

Copies of old coins are not considered "fakes" as it is the words on them that provide protective power, not the age of the coins.

"Literary" and "Martial" Divination —Spirit-writing is Alive and Well in Taipei

Offerings are made continually during the possession to ensure the *ji-tong*'s safety.

Among the most unusual sights in Taipei, of any kind, religious or secular, must be that of spirit possession (附身). It is most noticeably associated with a deity's anniversary celebrations or other important event, when young men invite possession then beat themselves with an assortment of weapons until blood flows, which is then used to write protective talismans and other esoteric charms. There is, however, a second form of possession, carried out early in the morning or late at night and behind closed doors, when groups of believers assemble and one or more of their number undergoes spirit possession, usually by their patron deity, who uses this human body as a tool to dictate long texts on religious or ethical topics.

As ever, there is great overlap, with the former characteristic of "martial divination" (武乩); the latter is known as "literary divination" (文乩).

1. Shock Troops of Martial Divination

The young men (and occasionally women) who offer themselves as tools of spiritual communication, are, as mentioned, known as *ji-tong* (乩童; divining youths; pronounced *dang-ki* in Taiwanese, the usual language of martial divination). One scholar refers to them as the "shock troops of local religion."*

Eyes half-open half-closed, their bodies move back and forward out of their control as possession begins. Minders steer them in the right direction or hand them the next implement, but generally they are left to follow their own volition or, rather, that of the spirit possessing them. Interested bystanders observe their movements to discern which deity or spirit has descended, and temple officials will note it down in their records.

---

* Daniel Overmyer.

Blood resulting from the self-flagellation is considered to be that of the deity not of the "divination youth" and may be used to write talismans. (above) Ferocious-looking weapons the *dang-ki* uses to beat himself. (bottom)

When clearly possessed, the *dang-ki* will be handed a series of ferocious-looking weapons such as a "shark sword" (鯊魚劍), "meteor hammer" (流星錘), dagger (短劍), metal whip (鋼鞭) or "wolf-tooth club" (狼牙棒).

One-by-one, he uses these to beat himself, mostly on the back, though some *dang-ki* will also strike their heads, stomachs or the sides of their torsos. Despite the ferocious appearance of the weapons and the exaggerated movements used in their application, blood loss is usually not excessive. In more extreme cases, in a single motion, the "youth" (though some may be quite elderly) will pierce himself through both cheeks using a sharp needle up to half a meter in length. The two ends of this needle are then pasted with talismans or, for experienced practitioners, hung with incense burners.

Bloody Messages and Spiritual Healing

Blood produced, considered to be that of the spirit not the man, is used by the possessed *dang-ki* to write talismans, which the faithful take away for personal protection or for *feng-shui* use in their homes. In former, less HIV conscious, times, small amounts of the blood would also be consumed by sick congregants or taken home for sick relatives.

Spiritual healing, particularly of psychiatric illnesses, is another popular aspect of a *dang-ki*'s work. Unscrupulous practitioners have, however, brought this side of the business into conflict with officialdom and received negative press coverage in recent years. It is not uncommon to see a *dang-ki* lay hands on a series of patients gathered specifically for this reason. Some temples, and some deities, specialize in this work.

2. Flying Peach-wood Pens of Literary Divination

At the other end of the spirit-possession spectrum, the atmosphere is refined, characteristic of its "literary" rather than "military" pretensions.

The temple is serene, men in rows on one side, women on the other, together, almost silently, murmuring a mantra. One woman beats a "wooden fish" drum, another strikes a giant bowl-shaped bell, eliciting rhythmic, sonorous heartbeats.

Before them on a raised platform, facing the altar and its selection of statues, flowers, fruit, candles and incense, is one of their number, similarly dressed in a blue robe. She holds a divining rod high above her head. Almost imperceptibly this double-handled rod with a carved dragon's head begins to sway back and forth, gaining in speed and amplitude, then suddenly turns downwards and begins to trace patterns in a sand-filled box.

"*Jiu*" (nine), calls out an attendant who has moved forward to look over her shoulder.

"Tian" (heaven), the words come slowly at first, then "*xuan*" (mystic), then "*nü*" (woman), then "*jiang*" (descends). The Mystic Goddess of the Ninth Heaven has descended (九天玄女降) and is present in the body of Ms. Lin, the woman at the stationary end of the dancing divining rod.

She will remember nothing of the next hour or so, but the words the Mystic Goddess uses her hands to trace in the sand will be called out by the "chanters of the phoenix" (唱鸞), written down by the "recorders of the phoenix" (錄鸞), announced to the assembled faithful, and later published as a booklet.

The temple falls silent as the goddess enters the participant's body.

This particular temple, the Jiu Zhong Temple (九重宮) in the hills above Nangang (南港), published one such book last year, a compilation of twelve teachings on filial piety (孝) and twelve on loyalty (忠), two of the central Confucian virtues.

Scenes such as this take place regularly in Taipei City, under the noses of its more straight-laced citizens, many of whom assume that such practices have long since disappeared or are only practiced in Tainan, Taiwan's "capital of superstitions."

In addition to transmitting "heavenly teachings," sessions like this also offer disciples personal advice, predictions and prognostications about their lives and spiritual progress.

Ancient Custom

Rituals calling down gods and spirits dates back at least to the Zhou dynasty when, apparently, the main function of music was to "make the gods and spirits come."* The dominant form of shamanism in China's early period involved spirit possession, in which a medium spoke a god's words for healing, prediction or moral instruction.

The temple keeps a record of its spiritual pact with a particular deity.

There is no evidence of spirit-writing, however, nor of whole books being dictated in this way. By the 5th century CE, however, young women, many concerned about the forthcoming silkworm season, were accustomed to asking yes-no questions of the Goddess Zi-gu (紫姑) on the anniversary of her death (15th day of the 1st lunar month). Although this did not initially include the provision of written predictions, by the Song dynasty (960-1279), Zi-gu was being credited with both elegant compositions and even paintings.

There are many references to her powers, including one by the poet Su Dongpo (蘇東坡; 1036-1101), who attended a Zi-gu séance at which the goddess composed ten short poems and then asked Su to record her appearance and make her name known.

In this way, the tradition evolved from a practice of illiterate women on the first full moon of the New Year, to male literati on a more frequent basis. Spirit-writing also expanded to include prognostications by other deities. Common appearances included Guan Gong, the red-faced god of knights, and Lü Dongbin (呂洞賓) of the Daoist Eight Immortals. Such figures were invoked to predict the outcomes of examinations, tell personal fortunes, bring rain or effect healings.

---

* Daniel Overmyer and David Jordan, *The Flying Phoenix*

Occasionally, they also offered moral and religious instruction, and it is this tradition that is particularly popular among the "literary diviners" (文乩) of Taipei today. Humankind having lost its understanding of the abstruse and mysterious truths, the spirit may make use of such sessions to "use the peach-wood pen to elucidate."

Astonishingly, this "pen" never hits the box sides despite dancing close to it on numerous occasions. It is made from both peach-wood (representing *yin*) and willow (*yang*).

Cold Turkey

Research by Overmyer and Jordan* suggests that true "wielding of the phoenix" (扶鸞; the name is said to have originated in ancient times, when the Lord of the Eastern Tree (東方木公) took on the appearance of a green *luan*

The peach-wood pen begins to move and trace out discernable characters in the sand tray.

---

* Daniel Overmyer and David Jordan, *The Flying Phoenix*

A young girl is possessed by the spirit and begins her training to become a "literary diviner."

(鸞; phoenix-like bird) to descend to earth) arrived in Taiwan around 1890, after which it was quickly assimilated by active local sects.

Spirit-writing was also closely connected, both on the mainland and here, with assisting in the cure of opium addiction through divine intervention. This was one important reason it remained popular in Taiwan, despite being outlawed by the Japanese administration in 1908.

That it is still alive and well in Taipei suggests that, whatever its basis in religion, superstition or group psychotherapy, spirit-possession and writing obviously still meet some deep need of a modern, educated, urban population.

Withdrawal

The session at the Jiu Zhong Temple ends with Mystic Goddess of the Ninth Heaven writing the word "withdraw" (退), after which Ms. Lin, the practitioner, stopped moving and was brought out of her trance by a spray of talismanic water administered by the master of ceremonies. A little while later, having changed into a print dress, she discussed the text she had delivered as though she herself had not been present. In her understanding of these events, of course, although the body had been hers, the presence was that of the goddess.

The words produced during a spiritual possession are recorded for future reference.

The scroll and seal symbolizing the contract between temple and patron deity are kept unopened on the main altar.

Chapter 6.

Museums and Shops

Religion in the City's Museums
—Ritual Implements and Works of Art

Placing an object in a museum sometimes ossifies it, but sometimes this new environment gives new context and sheds new light on a subject. Museums may also provide information about the historical background to religious practice that might be missing from a living temple, as well as providing better environments for the conservation of valuable items than smoke-filled temples.

The following are some of Taipei's museums, both public and private, which have significant religion-related artifacts.

1. Taiwan Folk Arts Museum (台灣民俗北投文物館)

Address: No. 32, YouYa Rd. (幽雅路), Beitou, Taipei City / Tel: (02) 2891-2318

The Taiwan Folk Arts Museum is housed in a category three historic relic on the slopes of Yangmingshan. As it attempts to cover all aspects of traditional culture, displays naturally include artifacts relating to Taiwanese religious practices and beliefs.

Ancestor worship, central to Han-Chinese religion, is represented by ancestral tablets and the portraits that predate today's use of photographs in clan shrines.

A fine collection of embroidery includes altar "skirts"(神桌裙) on themes including "The Eight Immortals Cross the Sea" (八仙過海), auspicious flower and animal symbols, and images of the "Three Stellar Gods" of Fortune (福), Prosperity (祿) and Longevity (壽). There are also "Eight Immortal Silks" (八仙綵) hung outside temples and homes on special occasions..

The museum has a number of fine altar paintings used in the Buddhist Ceremony of Water and Land (水陸道場畫) at which offerings are made to spirits in the afterlife.

There is also a rich collection of Aboriginal artifacts including decorated "shaman utensil boxes" used to hold the equipment used for divination and healing such as small knives, beads, piglet bones, and botanical remedies.

2. The Shung Ye Museum of Formosan Aborigines (順益台灣原住民博物館)

Address: No. 282, ZhihShan Rd. (至善路), Sec. 2, Taipei City / Tel: (02) 2841-2611

Religious connotations permeate all levels of traditional Aboriginal culture.

The Amis people made offerings to deities before and during pottery making, for example, as well as observing numerous taboos such as against laughing, swearing, breaking wind, and men and women living together, all aiming to prevent malicious spirits breaking pots during firing.

The intricate rituals accompanying every step of Tao (Yami) boat building, each in its correct season, means that the process from selecting a tree to launching the boat can take three years to complete.

The Tao group's "weapons" in this display are for fighting demons, not each other.

Atayal tattooing was not merely decorative, apparently, but done to help ancestral spirits recognize their clan descendents and find their way back to their tribal homelands.

The basement is dedicated to Aboriginal belief systems and spiritual life. Myths, divination and healing are all explained and related artifacts shown, culminating in an explanation of the religious aspects of head-hunting

3. National Taiwan Museum (國立台灣博物館)

Address: No. 2, XiangYang Rd. (襄陽路), Taipei City / Tel: (02) 2382-2699

Taiwan's oldest museum, dating from the beginning of Japanese rule (1895-1945), has extensive collections of historical religious statues, ritual implements, popular prints and books on religious themes and everyday utensils decorated with religious motifs.

The park surrounding the museum is also filled with historic relics and artifacts that it really constitutes a separate museum in its own right.

Of religious interest is the pair of *torii* (鳥居; bird residences) next to the northern fence. These are the archways that demarcated sacred land of Shinto temples from the profane world outside. The right-hand *torii* is inscribed 昭和十年十月, dating it to October of the 10th year of the *Showa* era (1926-64). The bases of the left-hand arch are strengthened with *kame hara* (turtle bellies).

The National Taiwan Museum is Taiwan's oldest museum, dating from the beginning of the last century.

4. Museum of the Institute of History and Philology, Academia Sinica (歷史文物陳列館)

Address: No. 130, Academia Sinica Rd., Sec. 2 (研究院路), Nankang, Taipei City / Tel: (02) 2652-3180

A genuine contender for the undiscovered gem of Taipei, this museum houses surprisingly extensive collections on a few specialist subjects. The display on anthropological research among the

Shang dynasty skulls on display at the Academia Sinica.

minority groups of southwest China includes much on indigenous religions but, unfortunately, is of little relevance to the "Religious Life of Taipei."

The same might be said of the Shang dynasty oracle bones and ritual bronzes, except that they represent a direct line to the divination techniques and acts of worship seen at any Taipei temple today, and also offer great insight into the ancient religious concepts of the Han-Chinese people that still underlie their beliefs and practices in the present day.

The collection of rubbings from Buddhist steles around China is a useful reminder of the important role this technique had in transmitting words and pictures before the invention of printing or photography.

Open: Wednesdays and Saturdays 9.30-4.30

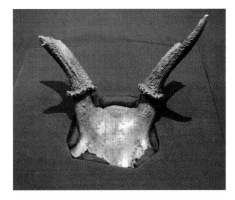

Deer skull bearing Oracle Bone Script.

5. The National Palace Museum (國立故宮博物院)

Address: No. 221, ZhiShan Rd. (至善路), Sec. 2, Shilin District, Taipei City / Tel: (02) 2882-1440

Without a permanent display dedicated to a religious theme (though Buddhist statues figure regularly), the NPM's main focus on religious artifacts is as artistic motifs spread fairly evenly through displays of painting, sculpture, calligraphy &c.

The bodhisattva Guanyin, Lao-zi, the Eight Immortals, human personifications of the Three Stellar Deities (Happiness, Prosperity and Longevity) are among the most commonly encountered.

Many items of jade had religious functions, providing a conduit for gods between heaven and earth, or protecting people, alive or dead, from evil spirits.

The collection of ancient bronze ritual vessels such as three-legged *jue* (爵), caldron *ge* (鬲) and *ding* for food offerings (鼎), are still found on altars and copied in pottery for decorative use.

Sets of bronze bells (鐘) and stone chimes (磬) dating from the 7-5th centuries BCE probably also had a religious function as "music originally intended to bring humankind closer to the gods."

Bronze *ding* decorated with animal mask design.

6. Museum of World Religions (世界宗教博物館)

Address: No. 248, ZhongShan Rd. (中山路), Yonghe (永和), Taipei County / Tel: (02) 8231-6666

A tour guide explains the cosmological symbolism in the MWR lobby.

Although the MWR attempts to present religious experience from around the planet, with its location in the Taipei suburbs and its founder a Chinese Buddhist monk, its strengths are definitely to be found in its displays of Buddhism, Daoism and "Religious Life of the Taiwanese."

While its design leans towards the experiential rather than doctrinaire, those wanting more than a minimum of information can access almost too much via the interactive computer screens placed before each display.

From the origin of Daoist priests' decorated headwear in the pins used to keep their hair in order, and the meaning of the Buddha's hand positions in a variety of Tibetan sculptures, to the punishments waiting wrongdoers in the ten halls of hell and the relevance of the seven stars on the sword in the mouth of the "Sword-biting Lion *Ba-gua*" used in *feng-shui*, nothing is omitted.

Each display contains some four-dozen artifacts, many much closer and, therefore, clearer than they are on a distant temple altar. A small sample of the other religions also reflect "Judaism in Taiwan," "Islam in China" and so forth.

7. The National Museum of History (國立歷史博物館)
Address: No. 49, NanHai Rd. (南海路), Taipei City / Tel: (02) 2331-1086

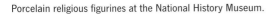

Unfortunately, this excellent museum has few displays of religious relevance. A number of 6th and 7th-century Buddhist statues greet the visitor, then there are a few ritual jades and bronzes, and some religious figures carved in jade hidden in a dark corner of the 3rd floor, though there are no English labels.

The NMH's strength is its pottery; the porcelain religious figures including Zhong-kui (the demon slayer), Li Tie-guai (one of the Eight Immortals), Arhats (Buddhist "saints"), Zhang Fei (patron deity of butchers) and others, do have English titles.

The best display, including detailed explanations, are those of Tang dynasty tricolor figurines, which the museum traces back to the use of funeral articles (俑), and, before that, to the burial alive of wives, servants and other necessary "possessions" at the funerals of important men.

Porcelain religious figurines at the National History Museum.

Shopping for Religious Artifacts

Although most temples sell incense, candles and joss money for burning on the premises, and talismans, charms and pictures for taking home, many visitors, moved by the experience, may wish to buy souvenirs of their visit or religious equipment for worship at home.

For such items, one needs to look for "Buddhist implement stores" (佛具店,) in the neighboring streets.

One good place with a wide selection is XiYuan Rd. (西園路) beside Longshan Temple (龍山寺). Superficially similar, some of the dozen establishments are more Buddhist, others more Daoist; some concentrate on home practitioners, others have everything needed to set up and run a medium-sized temple.

Guanyin gets her first coat of yellow paint.

Prayer cushion with lotus design.

1. Setting up an Altar

Those wishing to worship a favored statue can find everyone from Guan Di and Confucius, to a whole range of buddhas.

Small metal statues a few inches tall start at NT$300, wooden ones at NT$1-2,000. Sizes go as large as you like and, depending on the wood used and craftsmanship of the maker, prices go as high too. A two-foot-tall statue may cost NT$20-40,000. Believers can take them to a temple for consecration, which often involves addition of a talisman in a hole in the statue's rear.

2. Ancestor worship

If daily prayers to your ancestors appeals instead, wooden tablets (祖先牌) painted or inscribed with your family name and appropriately filial expressions, mounted in a glass case start from around NT$6,000.

3. Lord Tiger

Beneath the altar, you might like to place a model tiger. Representing Lord Tiger (虎爺), these start at NT$500 for a two-inch version, rising to around NT$2,500 for a foot-long tiger.

Lord Tiger, king (王) of the forest.

4. Censers, Cups, Candles and Lamps

Whether directed at Lord Tiger, your ancestral tablet, or deity of choice, worship generally includes wine poured into three cups, burning of incense in censers, and lighting of candles or lamps. All these are available, in numerous designs and sizes, and at varying prices. You can even buy a wooden altar, a glass picture depicting deity or auspicious design accompanied by vertical written panels (對聯; NT$2,000-20,000) and, for those of you planning to spend much time kneeling before the altar, a cushion embroidered with auspicious design.

5. Wooden Fish and Bowl Bell

Two musical instruments that adorn altars in Buddhist and Daoist temples alike and are used in ceremonies and when reading sutras are the "wooden fish" drum (木魚) and bell (鐘) in the shape of a bowl. These make good souvenirs and each cost from around NT$500 upwards. Cushions on which the instruments rest can be bought separately.

Wooden fish should be hit before purchase to check their sound.

6. Altar cloths

Embroidered "altar skirts" are often hung around the sides and front of the altar, while similar Eight Immortals cloths (八仙彩) hang from the ceiling or door lintel. Depending on the quality of work, these vary from NT$500 for a printed cloth to tens of thousands for beautifully executed pieces.

7. Prayer beads

Used for counting the repetitions of sutras or prayers, "recitation beads" (唸珠) are available in all manner of materials from wood to precious stones, and all manner of designs from smooth spheres to carved images of buddha heads. Various numbers of beads may also be used; Buddhist beads generally have 108 beads representing the 108 passions or karmic hindrances. Prices may be quoted per bead or per chain, and range from a few NT$ to thousands.

Brightly embroidered altar cloths can often be found at antique stores.

Prayer beads in the shape of *arhat* heads.

8. Home protection

Most stores sell a number of items connected with *feng-shui* (風水) protection of the home or office, such as *ba-gua* (八卦) trigram designs, usually with a mirror in the center (NT$200 upwards), "mountain and sea plaques" (山海鎮), "sword and lion plaques" (劍獅牌) and coin swords to be hung over the bed.

Some shops sell "dipper lanterns" (斗燈) used for promoting family fortunes, as well as the "treasured sword," scissors, steelyard, ruler, mirror, plate, umbrella and paper images of deities generally placed in them.

9. Divination

All the tools of divination are on offer, from "divination blocks" (筊杯) and sets of bamboo slips used to select a reading (籤; NT$400-2000), to turtle shells and coins (NT$1000 upwards), and a wide selection of reference books (in Chinese).

10. Self-flagellation

Those stores concentrating on temple supplies rather than those for home use, also sell a number of items used by *dang-ki*. Not recommended for personal use, ranging from hand-held "brushes" bearing sharp needles (NT$150) and two-foot-long multi-bladed weapons that look like mediaeval torture tools (NT$1500) to "meteor hammers" (流星錘) and "shark swords" (鯊魚劍) in which the teeth of some sea beast cut the flesh, these implements make interesting collectors' items.

Ba-gua designs and mirrors are the simplest, and cheapest, form of home protection.

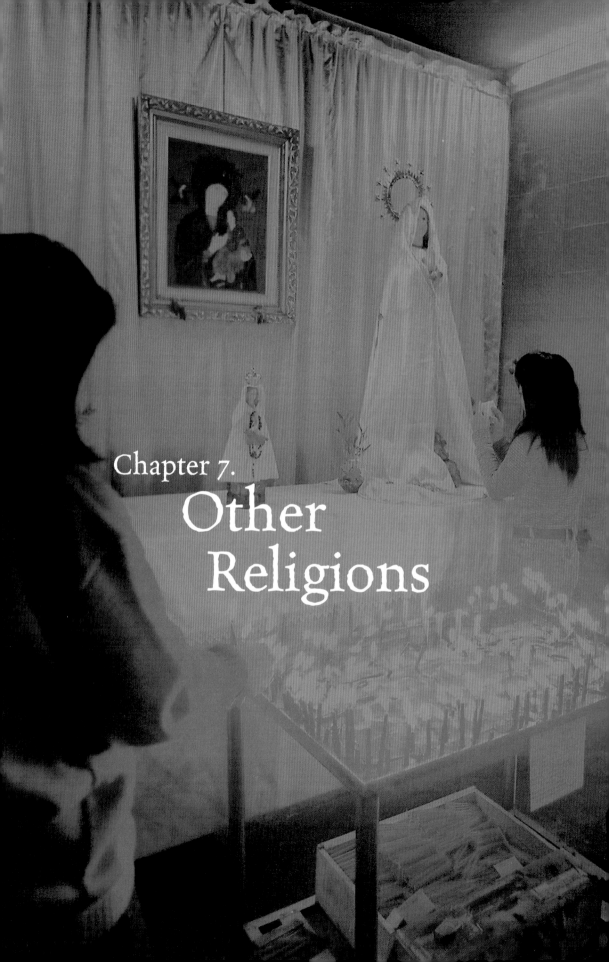

Chapter 7.
Other
Religions

Shinto — *The Way of the Gods*

Promotion of Shinto as the national religion during Japan's Meiji Restoration (明治維新; 1868-1912) had repercussions in Taiwan after cession to Japan in 1895.

Shinto (神道; Way of the Gods) is Japan's ancient religion of nature and ancestor worship, a polytheistic veneration of deities of mountains, rivers, trees and natural forces, of clan tutelary gods and the spirits of heroic individuals. As such, it has many similarities with China's indigenous pre-Daoist/pre-Confucian religious practices, many of which still existed in late imperial times.

Shinto has no founder, no official scriptures (the nearest things are, perhaps, the 8th-century collections of myths of the imperial family and other important clans), and no fixed doctrines. It does have ceremonies, prayers and festivals. Shinto might better be described as the underlying cosmic view and value system of the Japanese people rather than a religion in the Western sense. (Following introduction of Buddhism into Japan via China in the 6th century CE, Shinto's influence declined steadily. Shinto also absorbed many Buddhist ideas and practices.)

Shinto in Taiwan

Ironically, Taiwan's first Shinto shrine was dedicated in 1897 to Koxinga (鄭成功) the half-Chinese half-Japanese warlord who had become a Taiwanese hero for liberating the island from Dutch rule in 1661. By 1945 when the Japanese left, there were 68 government-accredited shrines around the country and 130 unofficial shrines. Most important was the Taiwan Shinto Shrine in Taipei, erected in 1901 and dedicated to the emperor's younger brother, Prince Kitashirakawa, who died of illness in Tainan in 1895 while commanding the Imperial Guards.

Its site is now occupied by the Grand Hotel. Most Shinto shrines were dismantled by the incoming KMT though some were converted into temples or, very commonly, to memorials to Chinese martyrs.

Today, there is scant reminder of this past. There are a few shrine entrance archways *torii* (鳥居; bird roosts) including a pair in the 2-28 Peace Park, and a preserved Shinto shrine on Hutou Shan (虎頭山) in Taoyuan.

Shinto was disestablished in Japan after the Second World War and most Shinto-practicing Japanese in Taiwan today belong to the Tenri (天理; Rule of Heaven) sect, which practices at home.

A number of Japan's "new religions" are also catching

Statue of Taiwanese hero Koxinga in place of honor in Hutou Shan's preserved Shinto temple.

on with Taiwanese people. These generally focus on some specific scripture or teaching, or combine elements of "Japanese religions" with elements of "foreign religions" such as Christianity.

It is unlikely that any Shinto shrines will reappear in Taipei in the near future, however.

Shinto *torii* archway dating from 1935 now finds a home in Taipei's 2-28 Peace Park.

Spirit tablet room in the Hutou Shan Shinto temple, which now functions as a shrine to Chinese martyrs.

Islam — "Submission to God's Will"

Islam in China

The first official Muslim visit to China is recorded as that of Sa'ad ibn Abi Waqqas in 650 CE, eighteen years after the prophet Mohammed's death, although Arabs had been trading in the region since much earlier. His visit, and the warm welcome offered to this new religion by the Tang emperor Gao Zong (高宗; r. 650-683), led to the establishment of China's first mosque, in the capital, Chang'an (長安). It still stands today.

Islam's crescent moon motif on the roof of the Taipei Grand Mosque. (Photo by Wang Neng-yu)

Muslims dominated the overland Asiatic trade routes between East and West, and, for a long time, the sea routes too. By the Song dynasty, Muslims more or less controlled China's imports and exports, and communities were well established in numerous provinces as well as the capital.

By the Ming dynasty, interaction and intermarriage had led to some sinicization, such as the adoption of Chinese names. Common examples include Ma (馬; for Mohammed), Mai (麥; for Mustafa), Mu (穆; for Masoud), Ha (哈, for Hasan), Hu (胡; for Hussain) and Sai (賽; for Sa'id).

Muslims also made great contributions to the development of Chinese astronomy, chemistry and other sciences.

The Qing court's policy of divide-and-rule, as well as the 17th-century conquest and 19th-century reconquest of Xinjiang with its large Uighur population, led to increased oppression of, and rebellion by, Muslims.

Today, China's Muslims number officially around 15 million, that is, a little over 1% of the population. These include around 8 million Hui (回), who tend to be more sinicized, 7 million Uighur and members of some eight other Islamic minorities. Unofficial estimates claim 20, 35 or even as many as 100 million Muslims.

Taipei's mosque, like others worldwide, is particularly busy on Fridays. (Photo by Wang Neng-yu)

Contrary to popular opinion, true Islam offers equality to women. (Photo by Wang Neng-yu)

Islam in Taiwan

Koxinga's relocation of troops to Taiwan in the middle of the 17th century is said to have included Muslim soldiers, but few traces remain today. Similarly, some 20,000 soldiers, civil servants and other Muslims arrived with the fleeing KMT in 1949.

Representing less than 0.5% of the population, Taiwan's Islamic community has struggled to maintain its identity and traditional practices. There are very few restaurants and butchers outside Taipei that sell *halal* meat, prepared in accordance with Islamic dietary laws.

The Taipei Grand Mosque, one of six mosques around the island, was built in 1960. It serves the religious needs of the 40% of Taiwan's 60,000 Muslims who live in Taipei, as well as visiting Muslims from all over the world, including the large population of Indonesian foreign workers. It includes features common to mosques all over the world, such as a domed

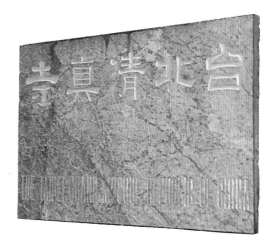

Welcome to the Grand Mosque, in Chinese, Arabic and English. (Photo by Wang Neng-yu)

Despite the fence, more and more people are visiting the mosque to find out for themselves the truth about Islam.

Detail of the mosque, built by architect Yang Chuo-cheng, who also designed the C.K.S. Memorial and Grand Hotel. (Photo by Wang Neng-yu)

salat (prayer) hall, *wudoo* (purification) room, minarets from which the faithful are called to prayer, arched gallery, and *mihrab* (prayer niche), which indicates the direction a worshiper must face during prayer.

The mosque (清真寺 in Chinese) has been frequently threatened with demolition due to disputes over land rights. It is now protected, due to designation as a religious heritage site by the Taipei City Government.

The city government has also approved a proposal by the Chinese Muslim Association (中國回教協會) to organize Islamic courses for schoolchildren during the summer vacation and to check information concerning Islam provided to all schools to eliminate stereotyping and misunderstanding.

In keeping with the fifth pillar of Islam, which stipulates that all able-bodied Muslims should make the pilgrimage to Mecca at least once in their lives. A number of Taiwan's Muslims participate in the *hajj* to Saudi Arabia each year. (The other four pillars are 1.) belief in only one god, Allah, 2.) prayer five times a day, 3.) charity and 4.) fasting during Ramadan.

Christianity — *Two Millennia Later on a Small Asian Island*

Taiwan is often described as being among the most religiously tolerant places in the world. Nowhere is this better seen, perhaps, than in the welcome given to foreign missionaries.

Initial Welcome

This warmth dates back to 635 CE when Alopen, a Nestorian from Syria, arrived in the Tang dynasty capital of Chang'an (長安), where he was provided with bed, board and assistants by the emperor, who referred to this alien faith as "The Luminous Religion." (景教). Alongside the blossoming of Buddhism in China, Nestorian Christians built churches and ministered to foreign merchants, missionaries and soldiers until 845, when the pro-Daoist emperor Wuzeng (武宗; r. 841-847) decided to expel all "foreign religions." Aimed primarily at Buddhism, it also curtailed the activities of Nestorians, Manichaeans and Zoroastrians. In any case, Chinese converts had been few.

Nestorians made a second attempt at converting the Chinese during the Yuan dynasty (1279-1368). Despite their own religious beliefs, the Mongolian rulers were tolerant and even subsidized

Christianity has come a long way since the first missionary came from Syria in 635 CE. (Photo by Hsu Yu-kai)

Christians represent around 3% of Taiwan's population.
(Photo by Hsu Yu-kai)

foreign missionaries. Nevertheless, Han-Chinese converts were again few.

The pope was invited to send one hundred well-educated missionaries but only one, John of Montecorvino, a Franciscan, arrived in Khanbalik (Beijing) in 1294. By the time of his death in 1328, he claimed to have made several thousand conversions but, as ever, most were foreigners or Mongols. Christianity disappeared with the ending of the Mongol dynasty in 1368.

The Rites Controversy

The Catholic Church, represented initially by Jesuits, appeared in the 16th century, followed a century later by Russian Orthodox chaplains who erected a church for Russian prisoners.

Recognizing the stability of Chinese culture, Jesuit missionaries wore scholars' robes, studied customs, scriptures, language and ideas, and were willing to adapt their own doctrines within reason. Using the prestige of Western science and technology to reach the literary class and court circles, they tried to persuade Chinese people that there were few differences between Christian teachings and Confucian ethical codes.

The Jesuit monopoly of missionary work in China ended in 1631 when the pope allowed Franciscans and Dominicans into the region. Their differing approaches led to disputes in China and repercussions back in Europe, in particular, concerning the Jesuit view that ceremonies honoring ancestors and Confucius were not religious and, therefore, that their practice by Chinese Christians was acceptable.

Dominicans denounced the Jesuits in what became known as the Rites Controversy and, in 1704, Pope Clement XI forbade Chinese Christians to participate in such rites. Emperor Kangxi (康熙; r. 1662-1722) was outraged and decreed that only missionaries supporting Ricci's practices could remain. By 1720, the golden age of Catholic missions in China was over.

"New" Christianity

Protestantism (新基督教 "New Christianity" as compared to Catholicism, 天主教 "Religion of the Heavenly Lord") initiated a

Despite the inclusion of English words, most churches are now thoroughly indigenized.

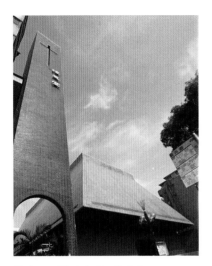

Modern... (Photo by Hsu Yu-kai)

fourth attempt at conversion in 1807, when the London Missionary Society sent Robert Morrison to Macau. To get around the 1720 ban, Morrison worked as a translator for the East India Company, which, unfortunately, meant the church became associated with the company's opium trading activities.

Morrison translated the Bible by 1819 and compiled the first English-Chinese dictionary, which became the standard for many years. (Taiwan's highest peak, Yu-shan (玉山), was named Mt. Morrison in English in his memory.) By his death in 1833, however, he had only ten Chinese Christian conversions to show for his efforts.

The Treaty of Nanjing (1842) ending the Opium War of 1839-1842 opened a number of coastal ports to trade, specified the right to preach and erect churches, and protected missionaries and Chinese Christians from Chinese laws.

Missionary activities were boosted and, by 1920, there were 8000 missionaries and more than 360,000 converts. By concentrating on "indirect evangelism" of education, medical care, orphanages (child baptisms were common) and relief work mainly in port cities, China became the largest missionary field in the world.

Sun Yat-sen (孫逸仙), "Father of the Nation," was a Christian; Generalissimo Chiang Kai-shek (蔣介石) became one in 1927. Many officials in the new republican government were Christians, and Christianity prospered in the anti-traditionalist atmosphere in the first decades of the 20th century, until the anti-Christian movement of 1922-27, which viewed missionary work as a vanguard of foreign imperialism and actually as an obstacle to China's own modernization. Missionaries left for safer postings, their number falling to 3,150 by 1928.

The communists' victory in 1949 heralded the end of missionary work in mainland China, as churches were forced to undergo the Three Self-Reforms Movement aimed at ridding them of imperialist, feudalist and bourgeois thinking. Many missionaries accompanied Chiang Kai-shek and the KMT to Taiwan; nearly all others were expelled by the early 1950s.

Christianity in Taiwan

Christianity was first brought to Taiwan in the 17th century by the Dutch (1626-61) and Spanish (1624-42) settlements. The Dutch Reformed Church sent some thirty ministers to Taiwan over forty years, while the Spanish sent around forty, mostly Dominicans and Franciscans.

The Dutch were particularly active among the Siraya group of plains Aborigines near today's Tainan, learning their language, customs and beliefs, setting up schools and churches, and baptizing several thousand people. Nevertheless, after expulsion from the islands by Koxinga's Ming-loyalist forces, all traces of Christianity disappeared.

Christianity reappeared after expansion of the Treaty of Nanjing in 1858 to include the ports of Keelung, Danshui and Kaohsiung in Taiwan. Catholics returned in 1859, English Presbyterians to southern Taiwan in 1865, and George MacKay of the Canadian Presbyterians to Danshui and the Taipei area in 1872.

Perhaps learning from earlier missionary experiences in China when mass conversions failed to achieve a lasting influence, Catholic missionaries initially adopted a more "qualitative" approach. By 1913, there were around 3,000 Catholic adherents; 8,000 in 1945; and around 300,000 in 1970.

Missionaries were particularly successful among the indigenous population, perhaps because of the egalitarian nature of their approach compared with the discriminatory policies pursued by the Japanese administration and the entrenched prejudices of the Han-Chinese majority.

... and traditional architecture make popular backgrounds for Christian couples posing for wedding photographs.

Today, around 100,000 of Taiwan's 370,000 Aborigines belong to the Catholic Church; while more than 95% belong to one or other Christian denomination.

English Presbyterians included William Campbell, who edited a dictionary of the Taiwanese language and initiated missions to the Penghu Islands and among the deaf; and Thomas Barclay, who founded the Taiwan Church Press in 1884 and translated the Romanized Taiwanese Bible.

In the north, the legacy of G.L. MacKay (1844-1901) includes Taipei's MacKay Memorial Hospital (馬偕醫院; surprisingly, originally named after a different MacKay), the Oxford College (forerunner of today's Aletheia University 真理大學), Dansui Women's School, sixty churches and

Rev. G.L. MacKay and assistants pulling teeth in northern Taiwan in the 19th century. (Photo from *From Far Formosa*)

clinics, some 2,400 converts and sixty native preachers, as well as more than twenty thousand pulled teeth, his preferred method of gaining a community's confidence.

Although MacKay and others had started to ordain native ministers, it was the expulsion of Western missionaries by the Japanese in the early 1940s that led to indigenization and autonomy of the Taiwanese churches.

The "foreigners' graveyard" in Danshui.

The C.K.S. Factor

Chiang Kai-shek's role as a Christian and his long-term support by the West meant that, at least for a while, Taiwan's Christians were in a favorable position after the KMT's arrival in 1945. The constitution of 1946/7 guaranteed freedom of assembly, association and religious belief, and the right to practice missionary work.

Nevertheless, the churches never had an entirely easy relationship with Taiwan's one-party state. The native Presbyterian Church (*Tai-oan Ki-tok Ti-lo Kau-hoe*), in particular, often found itself siding with opposition groups, usually inadvertently. The confiscation of two thousand Taiwanese-language Bibles in 1975, for example, was seen by Christians as a violation of human rights. In 1979, several ministers of the church were arrested as part of the government crackdown known as the Kaohsiung Incident. Earlier problems included expression of support for the P.R.'s admission to the United Nations by the World Council of Churches (to which Taiwan's Presbyterian Church belonged) and the Vatican, and Pope Paul VI's visit to Hong Kong rather than Taipei during his 1970 Asian tour.

Contextualization

Such problems are less critical in the atmosphere of plurality and democracy that have existed since the lifting of martial law in 1987. Issues of culture, nationality and sovereignty are still important, however, as debates begun by the Jesuits concerning contextualization still take center stage.

One of the main issues is leadership of the Church. As one pastor who has worked as a missionary in Taipei for over thirty years says, "For many years, the purpose of missionaries has been to work ourselves out of a job."

Not only are Taiwan's churches freeing themselves from foreign control and ideology to become truly Asian in outlook, but also, in an ironic twist, the Taiwan Presbyterian Church now sends its own missionaries to a dozen countries worldwide, including the USA and MacKay's homeland of Canada.

At present, Christians represent about 3% of Taiwan's population.

Tibetan Buddhism — Latest Import

Excitement around His Holiness the Dalai Lama's visits to Taiwan, the proliferation of Tibetan artifact stores and large sales of books by the Dalai Lama and other Tibetan teachers all point to Taiwan's current obsession with the Himalayan nation and its religion.

Is it a fashion accessory or something more; this year's trend or something that will last; if so, is it a threat to Chinese Buddhism or even Daoism, why is it happening now, and to what extent do Taiwanese people really understand the doctrines of that faith?

"Real Buddhism"

The adoption of Buddhist figures such as Śākyamuni (釋迦牟尼) and Guanyin (觀音) into Taiwan's "popular religion" (民間信仰) has tended to erode the identity of Chinese Buddhist schools and understanding of Buddhist teachings. One result is that Tibetan Esoteric Buddhism (祕教), although dating from some five hundred years later than initial developments in Chinese Buddhism, is often viewed as being closer to the original Buddhism of India.

Visiting Tibetan monks examine the Qing emperors' collection of Tibetan artifacts now preserved at the National Palace Museum.

"Daoist Department" of Buddhism

Tibetan Buddhism also has close parallels to some aspects of popular Chinese religious practice. Joseph Needham, referring to Esoteric Buddhism as the "Daoist department of Buddhism," wrote, "One can see at once that [it is]... a system of thought closely akin to the shamanist and magical side of ancient Daoism."*

Tibetan worship of personal gods, as well as magical elements such as *tantras* (late sacred texts on the borderline between Hinduism and Buddhism), *mantras* (words of power), *yantras* (talismans), mudras (hand gestures) and other charms aimed at warding off evil, make Taiwanese people feel at home with Tibetan religious practices.

In particular, Tibetan funeral ceremonies are becoming increasingly common. Over a seven-week period, *lamas* (monks) sit close to the corpse and read from the *Liberation by Hearing in the Intermediate State* (*Tibetan Book of the Dead*) to guide the spirit towards enlightenment or rebirth.

"Regarder of the World's Sighs"

The central role of the Bodhisattva Avalokiteśvara in Tibetan Buddhism, Taiwan's Buddhist schools, and even in popular Taiwanese religious practice is another important factor.

Known in Chinese as Guanyin (觀音; translation of the Indian meaning "Regarder of the World's Sighs"), Avalokitesvara is one of the most important figures in Mahayana Buddhism, embodying the ideal of compassion.

Both His Holiness the Dalai Lama and King Songsten-Gampo, who introduced Buddhism to Tibet, are regarded as incarnations of Avalokiteśvara, and his image is the most commonly used in Tibetan statues and *thanka* (paintings).

Many nominally "Daoist" temples in Taiwan similarly worship statues of this bodhisattva, most

* Joseph Needham, *Science and Civilisation in China, Vol II*, p.426

Tibetan *lamas* play traditional instruments during a religious ritual.

Under the watchful eye of the Dalai Lama, young monks spend several weeks making a sand *mandala*.

often of the eleven-faced thousand-hand variety, rather than the sexually provocative tantric style famous in Tibet in which a union of male and female symbolizes a union of compassion and wisdom.

In theory, this idea would give equal status to women but, as the Dalai Lama has said, Buddhist attitudes towards women, as well as Tibet's own imperialist past, may have contributed to the bad *karma* evidenced today by the invasion of his homeland by the Chinese.

Personal Mission

A final reason for the increasing popularity of Tibetan Buddhism in Taiwan is a change of heart by the Dalai Lama himself. Until recently, he tended to tar the ROC and PRC with the same brush, suspecting both of regarding Tibet as merely "a part of China." After his first visit to Taiwan, the Gelugpa group, which he heads, joined other sects in sending *lamas* to teach and perform ceremonies. There are now more than 2,000 such visits each year.

Dalai Lama fact file

* The title "Dalai Lama" is a transcription of the Mongolian Ta-le meaning "Ocean [of Wisdom], " plus Tibetan bla-ma meaning "higher one," a title conferred on spiritual teachers.

* There are around 6 million Tibetan people, though only around two million of these live in the Tibet Autonomous Region, where they are now outnumbered by Han-Chinese.

* The Chinese government says that 84,000 Tibetans were killed following its takeover of Tibet in 1950 and the fighting that led to the Dalai Lama's exile in 1959. The Dalai Lama's administration in India puts the figure as high as 1.2 million to date.

* The current Dalai Lama, Tenzin Gyatso, won the Nobel Peace Prize in 1989 and assumes a high-profile international political role.

* The "post" of the Dalai Lama has always been political since its inception five hundred years ago. Discovery of the Mongol ruler's great-grandson as the 4th Dalai Lama allied the Gelugpa sect to the Mongolian military power and helped bring unity to Tibet under Gelugpa leadership.

* Lhasa was founded in 639; the first Westerners were allowed to enter in 1904.

Index / Glossary